EUROPEAN MANAGEM

CW00705621

Training and development

EUROPEAN MANAGEMENT GUIDES
General editor: Pete Burgess

Recruitment
Terms and Conditions of Employment
Industrial Relations
Pay and Benefits

EUROPEAN MANAGEMENT GUIDES
General editor: Pete Burgess

Training and development

Incomes Data Services

Institute of Personnel Management

Phototypeset by The Comp-Room, Aylesbury
and printed in Great Britain by
Short Run Press Ltd., Exeter, Devon

British Library Cataloguing in Publication Data

Training and Development. – (European
Management Guides)
 I. Burgess, Pete II. Series
 658.3124

 ISBN 0-85292-455-0

The views expressed in this book are the author's own, and may not necessarily reflect those of the IPM.

Contents

General Introduction

European Management Guides

The growing involvement of British businesses in the European Community has imposed novel demands on managers. For many small and medium-sized companies the challenge has been to find new markets and consolidate service networks. Larger organizations have been swept up in a series of mergers, acquisitions, joint ventures, strategic reviews and rationalization. In both cases, managers with personnel responsibilities have seen their tasks expanded and redefined. Increasingly, this includes involvement, both direct and at arm's length, in the recruitment and management of employees in other member states of the European Community. In many organizations the human resource manager has become the key figure in integrating the individuals and cultures which make up an internationalized company.

Experience has shown, often painfully, that the management of people lies at the heart of whether an international joint venture, merger or acquisition succeeds or fails. And familiarity with the local culture and regulation of employment underpins any understanding of the opportunities and limitations facing key executives in a foreign subsidiary. Acquisitions in particular, with their inheritance of established employment law and industrial relations practices, can pose a special challenge to new management teams.

The European Commission's plans for new Community legislation on many aspects of employment, as a part of the 'social dimension' to the single European market, will bring national systems of employment law closer together. However, differences between cultures, institutions, law and practice will persist for the foreseeable future. Understanding and working with the grain of this diversity will be vital for any personnel or line manager entrusted with European responsibilities. Professional advice is indispensable in any European venture, but precious time and money can be saved by gathering information in advance before meeting lawyers, consultants or the local public authorities.

European Management Guides aim to meet this need for accessible and comprehensive information on employment in the countries of the European Community. The series, researched and written by Incomes Data Services Ltd, and published by the Institute of Personnel Management, consists of five handbooks covering:

- Recruitment.
- Terms and conditions of employment.
- Industrial relations.
- Pay and benefits.
- Training and development.

Each handbook presents information on a country-by-country basis, and is structured to allow easy cross-country comparison. Extensive appendices detail local organizations which can provide further help and information. European Management Guides are not, however, intended as a substitute for expert advice, tailored to an individual situation and given as part of a professional relationship. Every effort has been made to ensure that the information contained in the handbooks is accurate and relevant. The publishers and authors offer them to readers on the understanding that neither organization seeks to take the place of either a lawyer or a consultant.

Incomes Data Services

Incomes Data Services has monitored employment developments in Europe since 1974. IDS's International Service publishes:

- *IDS European Report*, a monthly subscription journal on pay and employment law and practice in existing and prospective member countries of the European Community. Each issue includes news on pay, collective bargaining and legal developments in Community countries, a Country Profile outlining recent developments in the employment and pay field, together with the economic background for individual countries, regular supplements on EC legislation and issues, features, and statistics on pay, labour costs and prices.
- *IDS International Documents*, two series of in-depth publications on an individual country basis covering (1) Recruitment and Dismissal and (2) Pay and Conditions. Updated regularly, each series provides context and detail for a single country in these crucial areas of human resource management.
- *1992: Personnel Management and the Single European Market*, published jointly with the Institute of Personnel Management.

For more details please contact: IDS Subscriptions, 193 St John Street, London EC1V 4LS (tel. 071-250 3434, fax 071-608 0949)

Acknowledgements

This handbook was researched and written by the International Department of Incomes Data Services Ltd, London. The series editor is Pete Burgess, and contributions were also prepared by Angela Bowring, Andrea Broughton, Sally Marullo, Tony Morgan, Stephen Steadman, George Tsogas and Caroline Welch. The authors would like to thank Frederick Geers (VDAB, Brussels), João Conde (Selgec, Lisbon), Janice Caplan (Scala Associates, London) and Marco Sonnino (Genoa). Thanks are also due to the panel of expert advisers, drawn from the national committees of the IPM, and the staff of the IPM's Publications Department.

Introduction

Training and development in Europe

This is the fifth, and final, volume in the IPM–IDS series of European Management Guides. It provides a broad description of the systems of education and vocational training in each of the countries covered, and as such complements the first book in the series, which deals with recruitment. The main areas covered are:

- Secondary and higher education.
- Initial vocational and technical education.
- The education of managers.
- Statutory and agreed time-off rights for employees.
- Funding arrangements.

Education and training in the European Community are marked by a high degree of diversity at the level of public institutions and formalized training systems. If there is any trend towards a convergence of practice, it is evidenced in the interest shown in the 'German model' in a number of countries, especially those seeking to overhaul existing training arrangements. Best practice in areas such as management training or development also exhibits a number of common features rooted in general human resource management principles. However, these too are shaped by local customs, such as the typical degree qualifications held by managers – generally more closely tied to occupation in continental Europe than in the UK – and typical career trajectories. Overall, individuals tend to stay with companies much longer in continental Europe, with job-hopping largely confined either to countries experiencing rapid growth against a background of managerial shortages, as in Portugal and Spain, or in sectors where the demand for specialists outstrips supply. Both phenomena have abated with the onset of recession.

Differences between the UK and continental Europe

Beyond this, there are some common features which offer points of contrast between 'typical' continental practice and the exercise and philosophy of education and training in the UK.

Funding and mandatory training. A number of countries – notably France – have mandatory levies (either agreed or statutory) to ensure that minimum levels of training expenditure are complied with. In Germany the training services provided by chambers of trade and commerce are partly covered and partly subsidized by the membership fees, and membership is compulsory for companies in most areas of business. In Greece there is also a levy of 0·45 per cent of wage costs, collected through the social insurance system and paid into a fund to be jointly administered by unions and employers.

However, the existence of a levy exacted if firms spend below a required percentage of their pay bill on training, as in France, does not necessarily ensure either that training is undertaken or that courses meet the training needs of employers and employees. In France, for example, it has been reported that small and medium-sized companies sometimes prefer to pay the levy rather than offer continuing training to employees who are then better equipped to move on to larger organizations. In contrast, in Germany – which has no mandatory training requirements for companies – a well developed training culture, with strong employers' organizations and unions actively supporting training, and a perception of training which equates it more with capital investment than with wage costs, have ensured that there is an oversupply of training places in the west.

The institutional context of training. Countries with a strong education and training record typically integrate training with the upper level of secondary education. This can take the form of a requirement that people under 18 must continue to receive some general education, as in Germany, where a part of the theoretical training under the 'dual system' includes a broad educational component. Alternatively, as in the Netherlands and Denmark, the bulk of initial training is carried out within the public education system, as one option in a variety of secondary school choices. The UK is one of the few countries in Europe to have comprehensive education at both lower and upper secondary levels. In Belgium, Germany and the Netherlands, for example, school students enter either vocationally orientated or academically orientated institutions or streams on entering secondary school – although with much greater scope for interchange than there was between the old UK grammar and secondary modern systems. Indeed, in Germany a number of school students in possession of an *Abitur* certificate entitling them to enter university choose initially to take an apprenticeship because of its subsequent benefit in pursuing a technical career.

Moreover, in many countries possession of a vocational or technical qualification can serve as a basis for entry into higher education. This closer integration between education and initial training, and the award of a recognized vocational qualification at the end of school education, not only introduces a more systematic element into vocational training but also represents a major investment in basic and intermediate skills, expressing both a social commitment to young people and an effort to raise the status of vocational training. However, although it raises and broadens the general level of skills, and undoubtedly contributes to subsequent occupational flexibility, this approach can suffer from a degree of detachment between the vocational courses offered in specialized schools and the real world of commerce and industry. As a result, a number of countries have been exploring ways of bringing formal training and work closer together, either by encouraging more apprenticeships (as in France) or restructuring curricula and involving industry and unions in the structuring of courses.

University and tertiary education. The UK's comparative weakness in providing high-quality training for the 16–19 year age group contrasts with a relatively strong performance at tertiary level. Tertiary education in most of continental Europe differs markedly from that in the UK. UK A levels function as a notable barrier to the more limited number of university places on offer. In most of the rest of Europe a larger proportion of the school population obtains an advanced school leaving certificate (such as the *Abitur* in Germany or the *baccalauréat* in France) and universities, in general, offer open enrolment. Moreover, there is less specialization in this age group, and virtually all university entrants are required to have studied a foreign language and a science, maths or technical option to the age of 18–19. Selection based on exam results (*numerus clausus*) is usually confined to specific disciplines, and, apart from the special case of the *grandes écoles* in France, is not used to assign candidates to higher or lower-status universities. Entry ratios into tertiary education in the UK (that is, the ratio of first-time entrants into tertiary education as a percentage of the relevant age group) are among the lowest in Europe. Some 6 per cent of 18 year olds enter non-university tertiary education and 15 per cent enter university education in the UK. This compares with total entry ratios of 36 per cent in France, 28 per cent in Germany, 28 per cent in Italy and 30 per cent in the Netherlands.

However, the more restrictive entrance into tertiary education is matched by a much lower drop-out rate in the UK. Whereas only 31 per cent of Italian students and 55 per cent of French students are still in higher education at the time when degrees are typically taken, the corresponding ratio for the UK is 94 per cent (90 per cent for men and 99 per cent for women), by far the highest survival ratio in the European Community. The net effect is to produce a graduation rate for the UK which broadly matches that of most other EC member countries, though with qualifications which generally require a shorter study period.

The dash for MBAs seen in the USA, the UK and to some degree Spain has not, or at least not yet, been emulated to the same degree elsewhere in Europe. Only a handful of European universities offer MBAs, and then frequently in association with American universities and sometimes not legally recognized within the indigenous system of qualifications. MBAs are often principally sought by graduates hoping to enter consultancy or seeking to round off a technical education before entering management. A number of factors lie behind this. In France and Germany the existing standard of pre-entry management education tends to be very high: graduates will have at least four to six years of higher education, often in rigorous disciplines such as engineering or engineering combined with business studies. There is virtually no tradition in Europe of liberal arts graduates entering management and subsequently looking for a formal management qualification. Moreover, graduates have tended to stay longer with the organization into which they were recruited. Although this has undoubtedly weakened over the past decade, relatively low levels of management turnover have meant less demand for a qualification which enables the holder to enter and re-enter the executive labour market.

Lower levels of interest in MBAs does not mean, however, that post-entry management education is neglected in continental Europe. Short courses and seminars are provided in profusion, both in-house and by consultancies, private universities and public training agencies (a market in which UK business schools have been very active in Europe). And most surveys suggest that the lion's share of continuing training budgets in Europe is used in management and supervisory training.

European Community training initiatives

Under the Treaty of Rome (article 118), the European Commission is entrusted with the task of promoting co-operation between member states in the areas of basic and advanced vocational training. Article 128 also requires the Council of Ministers to lay down general principles for implementing a 'common vocational training policy' whose role is to contribute to the 'harmonious development of . . . national economies and the common market'. The European Social Fund, established under article 123 of the Rome treaty, makes funds available for measures intended to promote geographical and occupational mobility, and specifically for vocational retraining.

The organization responsible for Commission activities on training is Task Force: Human Resources, Education, Training and Youth, established within the social affairs directorate, DG5 (see below). Research and co-ordination of information-gathering on education and training are carried out by a separate agency, the European Centre for the Development of Vocational Training (CEDEFOP), located in Berlin. European Community efforts in the field of vocational education and training have taken practical shape in four main areas:

- Mutual recognition of professional qualifications.
- Comparability of vocational qualifications.
- A broad range of exchange and other programmes, some of which are intended to help realize the aims of mutual recognition, together with the establishment of a number of databases on training and education. (Details of training and exchange programmes can be obtained from the Employment Department; see below.)
- Support for training in individual member states through the European Social Fund. (See, for example, chapter 9 below.)

With the exception of grants and contributions to training schemes through the Social Fund, most of these programmes have been aimed at improving the mobility of labour rather than shaping or harmonizing national training arrangements. Moreover, whereas the programme for the mutual recognition of professional qualifications has culminated in directives imposing obligations on member states, activities in the field of comparability of vocational qualifications are intended to provide information: for example, there is no requirement on an employer recruiting workers to accept a vocational qualification awarded in another EC country as equivalent to a national qualification.

Mutual recognition of professional qualifications

The European Community has adopted two broad approaches in seeking to enhance the free movement of professionally qualified people within the Community. They are termed the 'sectoral approach' and the 'general approach'. The sectoral approach represented the first method by which the Community sought to guarantee free movement. Under it the European Community compared the education and training of individual professions in each member state, then attempted to harmonize them across the entire Community. Member states must restrict entry to the selected professions to individuals with a qualification which meets the harmonized standard. Any individual holding such a qualification is entitled to have it recognized in other member states. The outcome has been a series of directives for specific professions: at present, they cover doctors, nurses, vets, midwives, pharmacists and general practitioners. Architects have been subject to a slightly different approach under which member states are required to recognize any architectural qualification of degree standard provided it covers the fields set out in the directive and lasts for a specified minimum duration. This approach has been seen as protracted and complex: seventeen years were required to agree the directive on architects, for example.

In 1985 the Commission moved to a broader procedure, under which qualifications covering all 'regulated professions' would be recognized by all member states in fields requiring at least three years' university-level education (or the equivalent). In the UK the term 'regulated professions' includes those directly regulated by the state but more commonly by professional bodies operating under royal charter. The professions covered include accountants, chartered engineers, barristers and solicitors, a number of forms of recognized therapy, and teaching. The approach was embodied in Directive 89/48/EEC, adopted by the Council of Ministers in December 1988, with implementation from January 1991. (Member states have been proceeding with implementation during 1991–2: the Directive will also apply in EFTA countries from 1993). The system operates through the regulating bodies, who are required to examine qualifications and accept applications subject to a number of safeguards. Firstly, if the length of training received by an individual in one member state is shorter than in the country they wish to work in, the regulating body can ask for evidence of up to four years' experience as a fully qualified professional. Secondly, if there are differences in the content of curricula, incoming professionals can either take an examination to verify their ability or undergo a period of up to three years' supervised practice. In most professions the individual may choose how to demonstrate the capability to exercise his or her profession. However, in occupations involving a detailed knowledge of national law the member state can impose a procedure. In the UK the regulations implementing the directive are the responsibility of the Department of Trade and Industry (see below).

This approach has now been extended to regulated occupations, admission to which requires a qualification (diploma, certificate) obtained after one to three years' study. In the UK this would embrace a number of occupations accredited as National Vocational Qualifications (SVQs in Scotland) at levels 3 and 4. Directive 92/51/EEC was adopted in June 1992 and is due to be implemented by June 1994. At the time of writing, implementation procedures were still at an early stage.

Comparability of vocational qualifications

In contrast to EC initiatives in the field of professional qualifications, which impose requirements on member states to provide for recognition, since 1985 the Community has been preparing comprehensive information material on the comparability of vocational qualifications. The work is co-ordinated by CEDEFOP, the EC's training agency in Berlin (see appendix below), drawing on national bodies (who in turn consult employers' organizations, trade unions and training authorities). The main aim of the exercise is to enhance workers' freedom of movement by enabling them, and prospective employers, to gauge the status of qualifications for a range of skilled jobs, grouped by sector. Nineteen industrial and commercial sectors were selected for examination, and the results for all are expected to be published in the EC's *Official Journal* by the end of 1992, each time as a separate publication. (Information sheets on specific trades are available in the UK from the Employment Department, see appendix.) For each job description – for example, twenty occupations were tackled in the metalworking industry – the procedure examines the title (and in some cases the level) of the qualification (in the original language and in translation), the institutions providing training and the organizations awarding the qualification.

Euro-qualifications

'Euro-qualifications' is a new programme, also aimed at enhancing freedom of movement for workers, set to run from 1992 to 1994. It aims to give a European dimension to vocational qualifications and training programmes in thirteen vocational areas (in the UK they include hotel and catering, telecommunications, textiles, transport, graphics and languages). Within each area four occupations will be selected and a common job profile agreed. The next stage is to identify existing vocational qualifications, and examine how differences between national training levels and contents can be bridged. One proposal is to develop training modules to fill gaps, and enable individuals to move between countries (for example, through language training and preparation for working abroad). The project is organized in the UK by DALI (see appendix).

Appendix: addresses

Task Force: Human Resources, Education, Training and Youth: Rue de la Loi 200 B-1049 Brussels Belgium

CEDEFOP Jean-Monnet-Haus Bundesallee 22 1000 Berlin tel. + 49 30 88 41 20

Employment Department Qualifications and Standards Branch Moorfoot Sheffield S1 4PQ tel. 0742 594123 fax 0742 758316

Employment Department European Training Policy Branch Room 339 Caxton House Tothill Street London SW1H 9NF tel. 071-273 5400 (For details of EC training and exchange programmes see too *Employment Gazette*, June 1991, pp. 354–9.)

National Council for Vocational Qualifications 222 Euston Road London NW1 2BZ tel. 071-387 9898

Scottish Vocational Education
Council
Hanover House
24 Douglas Street
Glasgow G2 7NQ
tel. 041-248 7900

Department of Trade and Industry
Internal European Policy Division
1 Victoria Street
London SW1 0ET
tel. 071-215 5610

DALI
388–96 Oxford Street
London W1R 1FE
tel. 071-491 8533

Chapter 1

Belgium

Education and training have been divided along linguistic and regional lines for some time. Following the 1988 constitutional reforms, almost all responsibility for educational matters was transferred from central government to the regions. Only the length of the period of compulsory schooling and the minimum standards set for qualifications and diplomas, together with issues such as statutory paid educational leave, are still under the control of central government. Vocational training was devolved along linguistic lines in 1980, allowing a considerable degree of local financial responsibility, with full local financial devolution from 1988. The right to education in one's native language is a fundamental right and freedom in Belgium; laws passed as early as 1932, and amended in the 1960s, established an almost complete linguistic division. There are virtually no bilingual schools. Each of the regions has its own education ministry as well as its own training and employment organization. For Flanders and the Flemish-speaking community it is the VDAB (Vlaamse Dienst voor Arbeidsbemiddeling en Beroepsopleiding), which is responsible for training and job placement issues. The same functions are carried out for Wallonia and the French-speaking community by FOREM (Office communautaire et régional de la formation professionelle et de l'emploi), which also lends some support to the German-speaking community. In general, traditional private education is more prevalent among the Flemish-speaking community, whereas public education is stronger in the French-speaking community.

A number of national and regional bodies involved in policy and planning for education and training involve both employers and trade unions: they range from the National Labour Council to company works councils. Both FOREM and VDAB have representatives of employers and trade unions on their management boards. Given the steady rise in unemployment (over 11 per cent at the beginning of 1992), training and development to enable reintegration into the labour market have become an important political issue. On the other hand, employers are becoming increasingly worried about the possible effects of early retirement policies introduced in 1991 – allowing men to retire at 60 instead of 65 – which have already begun to encourage experienced employees to leave the labour force at a time when there are fewer young entrants. This concern has been increasingly reflected in the attention paid to training issues in collective bargaining.

The education system

Under the Education Amendment Act, 1983, full-time education is compulsory for all children aged between 6 and 16, and part-time education until the age of 18. In order to qualify for official recognition and state subsidies, schools – which may be publicly or privately run – must conform to the basic legal guidelines governing curriculum, structure and class size, and must submit to state inspection. No external examinations are carried out at any level. All certificates, diplomas and other qualifications are issued by the individual school, provided the school conforms with government standards and regulations. In primary schools certificates are issued by teachers, in secondary schools by class councils, and in higher education they are issued by boards of examiners. In cases where school standards are found wanting, a warning is issued by the state inspectors, and in extreme cases school certificates may be de-recognized.

Secondary education

In looking at the system of secondary education, it is important to distinguish between the various curricular options, on the one hand, and the specific system (or 'type') on the other. The curricular options, which tend to be taught in schools specializing in one curriculum with its implicit selection, are as follows:

- General secondary education (ASO) is customarily intended as preparation for university education.
- Technical secondary education (TSO), which combines general education and more technical training.
- Art education (KSO), which mixes general education with an arts emphasis.
- Vocational secondary education (BSO), which provides specific vocational training.

The TSO and BSO curricula provide the main system of initial vocational training for technical, skilled and semi-skilled workers.

At the end of the ASO, TSO and KSO courses – after six years – a certificate is awarded by the school which entitles the student to move on into higher education (see below). Certificates are of various types, and are validated by a number of bodies (including the universities themselves). It is possible to gain entry to higher education through the BSO course, although it requires an additional year's schooling.

Since 1971, there have been two systems of secondary schools: the so-called Type I ('renewed education') and Type II (traditional education). Both types encompass the choice of courses outlined above, but Type I schools enable students to transfer more easily from one course to another in the first two years. The Type II system, which is more widespread in the Dutch-speaking community, divides secondary education courses into two cycles of three years: lower and upper secondary education. Schools will usually offer at least two of the curricula set out above, but rarely all four. The KSO (art education) course begins in the fourth year, after three years' general education.

Type I education is divided into three cycles of two years, with a first-year curriculum common to all. Selection between ASO, TSO, KSO and BSO is made after the second year, although some vocational training begins in the second year. The courses last a total of six years, with the additional seventh year for BSO pupils wanting to go on to higher education. Students who leave full-time education at the age of 16 are required to carry on some form of part-time education until they are 18. It is only at that stage that they will receive any full qualification, although part-time attendance leads to a lower qualification.

As of the 1989/90 academic year in Flanders a combination of Type I and II education was introduced on an experimental basis. This *Eenheidsstructuur* will completely replace Type I and II education in 1994/95. It is to consist of three two-year cycles, with optional elements depending on the course chosen by the student. In the academic year 1988/89 there were a total of 825,000 pupils attending secondary schools in Belgium (of whom 55 per cent were in Flanders and the remainder in the French and the small German-speaking communities). By curriculum, 56 per cent were in general secondary education, 21 per cent in vocational education, 22 per cent in technical education and 0·3 per cent in arts education. (The percentage following general education was higher in the French-speaking areas.)

Approximately 20 per cent of the relevant age group move into some form of higher education (cf. 15 per cent to university and 21 per cent into tertiary education, all told, in the UK). However, problems of definition of the institutions led the OECD to conclude that the Belgian data probably underestimated the true proportion.

Higher education

Like secondary education, higher education, both university and non-university, is controlled largely by the regions and divided along linguistic lines. Legislation from 1970 classified higher education into universities, on the one hand, and a variety of other educational institutions offering more vocationally orientated courses in economics, agriculture, the paramedical professions, the arts, teacher training and technical subjects. Entry to all forms of higher education requires a certificate of secondary education, with universities generally requiring a diploma of proficiency (*diplôme d'aptitude/bekwaamheidsdiploma*). These qualifications are generally awarded by the individual schools, although in the French-speaking community there is also a Central Examining Board which is entitled to award such diplomas.

University-level education is available at seventeen universities and other institutions of higher education, both state and private. There are six full universities in Belgium: three are French-speaking (Université de l'Etat à Liège, Université Libre de Bruxelles, Université Catholique de Louvain) and three Flemish-speaking (Rijksuniversiteit te Gent, Vrije Universiteit Brussel, Katholieke Universiteit te Leuven). In addition, the Université de l'Etat à Mons and the Universiteit Antwerpen offer a more limited range of university courses. An initial diploma (*candidat/kandidaat*) is awarded after two or three years' undergraduate study, followed by a degree (*licencié/licenciaat*) after a further two or three years' study and the submission of a thesis. Second-stage qualifications usually grant the right to practise a recognized profession. Doctorates take a further minimum of one to two years, and usually considerably longer.

Non-university higher education. Institutions in this sector offer either short courses (one cycle of two to three years) or long courses (two cycles of at least two years). Entry requirements for short courses vary considerably, and offer more vocationally based training, with courses in fields such as nursing, social work or primary school teaching. Long courses are considered to be on a par with university education, and the admission criteria are much the same as for universities. Over the past ten years there has been an increase in the number of non-university students in higher education, with 65 per cent following short courses and 35 per cent on long courses. Although a number of higher education institutions offer MBA courses, reflecting the absence of business schools, these are not in great demand.

According to OECD figures for 1988, 61 per cent of those enrolled in universities complete their degree to *licencié* level (compared with 94 per cent in the UK).

Vocational training

School students who leave school at 16 are obliged to carry on part-time education until the age of 18. Such study ranges from 240 to 360 hours a year, depending on age and the point in the academic year at which the part-time course is taken up. The bulk of initial vocational training is carried out on the TSO and BSO courses in schools. Students who leave full-time education at 16 can continue TSO, or more commonly BSO, courses on a part-time basis. There are a number of centres specifically for part-time education up to 18 years and they are frequently attached to schools offering only technical or vocational (TSO/BSO) courses: some forty-eight such centres exist in the Flemish community, forty in the French-speaking community and two in the German-speaking areas. Upon completion of part-time courses, students receive a certificate of proficiency.

Initial vocational training may also be completed under an apprenticeship scheme, combining part-time education and vocational training with employment. They include vocational training in conjunction with an apprenticeship – either an industrial apprenticeship or a craft apprenticeship under the auspices of the regional organizations or a work placement. Vocational training is administered almost entirely along linguistic lines, and falls under the control of the VDAB in Flanders and the FOREM in Wallonia. A number of training courses are run at vocational training centres under the auspices of VDAB or FOREM, or they can take place at more general educational centres, in collaboration with a number of companies or as in-house company training.

Apprenticeships and basic training

Most apprenticeship contracts are regulated closely by legislation. They are usually for craft training and for the self-employed professions (and known as *formation permanente des classes moyennes/vlaams instituut voor het zelfstandig ondernemen*), a category embracing a wide range of service and skilled manual occupations. These are aimed at young people of at least 16 years of age who have completed a minimum of two years' full-time secondary education, with a view to a career in small or medium-sized companies. The apprenticeship contracts run for a minimum of one year up to a maximum of three years, although under regional law for the French-speaking community this period may be extended by one year if required. Training consists of twenty-eight hours per week within the company in the first year, and thirty-two hours per week in the second and third years, as well as more theoretical training of 120 hours per year. Apprentices are required to pass a medical exam before undertaking the apprenticeship and again within the first six months. Certain conditions are also imposed by law on the employers. They must, for example, be at least 25 years old (lowered to 23 if the employer holds a managerial diploma) or have six years' experience in their profession. An apprentice is entitled to time off in lieu for non-working days spent in training; pay is determined by collective agreement and is index-linked.

Industrial apprenticeships

Industrial apprenticeships (*apprentissages pour travailleur salarié/ industrieele leercontracten*) are governed by legislation introduced in 1983. It does not apply to companies with fewer than fifty employees, and embraces the 18–21 year old age bracket, as well as the under-18s. Industrial apprentice contracts are signed for a minimum of six months and a maximum of two years, although the period can be extended by agreement in some professions. Apprentices, who have part-time worker status, are paid the industry minimum for a worker of equal skill, *pro rata* for hours worked. At the end of the apprenticeship they receive a certificate of completion detailing the periods of training and the content of the programme. Industrial apprenticeships are monitored by the works council in the company. Apprenticeship committees are also set up by the joint industry boards (*paritaire leercomités*). Unions and employers are both represented on these committees, and they are charged, among other things, with designing training programmes, organizing examinations and setting the recognition standards for apprenticeship qualifications. They are also empowered to establish the terms and conditions of apprenticeships in companies, largely through collective agreements. These may specify the maximum number of apprentices in a given firm, recommend training centres and detail the division of costs among employers taking apprentices on. The take-up of industrial apprenticeships has been lower than was expected when the law was passed. This has been attributed in part to the low recognition accorded to these qualifications.

Continuing training

Continuing and higher vocational training is provided in-house and also with frequent resort to public institutions (organized along linguistic lines). The services of the latter are set out below. Companies tend to use such services to provide general training, and to complement initial training, whilst keeping more advanced technical training (which may be product-specific) in-house. In a recent survey of continuing training carried out by CEDEFOP, the European Centre for the Development of Vocational Training, the companies interviewed had all developed a range of continuing training plans, covering short, medium and long-term needs. Expenditure on continuing training within the companies surveyed ranged from 3·5 to 8 per cent of the pay bill (with the highest percentage in a pharmaceutical company's high-technology research centre).

Work-training contracts

A law dating from 1987, and amended in 1989, allows companies to offer work-training contracts (*conventions emploi-formation/ overeenkomsten werk-opleiding*) to employees aged between 18 and 25 years, provided the employees do not hold a higher education diploma or a certificate of technical secondary education. To encourage employers to offer this advanced vocational training, their social security contributions are temporarily reduced for this category of employee. The employee must work at least half normal hours but no more than full-time hours less total training hours. The law stipulates the type of training permitted within the contract: it includes courses run by part-time educational centres (see above), short or long-term higher education evening classes, managerial training and courses run or recognized by VDAB or FOREM. Training must run for a minimum of one year and a maximum of three years, with at least 500 hours per year (except for managerial/supervisory training, which is set at 256 hours per year).

Work placement

Primarily as a means of reducing youth unemployment, legislation was introduced in the mid-1970s which obliged employers to provide a certain number of work placements (*stages*) for people under 30 who had no more than six months' employment behind them. The legislation stipulates that firms with a work force of more than fifty must take on a number of *stagiaires* equal to at least 3 per cent but no more than 4 per cent of the work force. Companies with under fifty employees need provide no more than three work placements. For the purposes of the law a number of apprenticeships are considered to be work placements, including the industrial apprenticeships dealt with above. Work placements generally last six months or twenty-six weeks, and may be extended by a further six months. Pay for a *stagiaire* is set at 90 per cent of the salary of a worker of equal skill. A number of financial incentives also encourage employers to take on a *stagiaire* permanently – including pay for the first year set at 90 per cent of normal pay for a worker of equal skill and a reduction in the employer's social security contributions for the second year of employment. In 1990 there were a total of 24,905 work experience placements in the private sector and 9,465 in the public sector.

Advanced vocational training also exists for crafts and self-employed professions, along much the same lines as the work placement training described above. A number of large industries, notably metalworking, textiles and the construction industry, operate their own training centres for developing advanced sectoral skills. Individual companies, particularly smaller ones, make frequent use of the centres and training facilities for advanced training run by the VDAB/FOREM (see below).

FOREM and VDAB vocational training

Constitutional changes aimed at linguistic devolution led to a restructuring of the National Employment Office, which used to deal with all training and employment matters, and a shift of its powers to regional and community offices: FOREM and VDAB (see above). Both are administered by joint management committees under the control of executive councils. The VDAB was set up in 1984, with further powers devolved in the 1988 reforms. FOREM was not established until 1988, and some of its services are still not fully established or operational.

Both FOREM and VDAB are organized along the same lines, operating their own vocational training centres, centres run in co-operation with companies, and general education centres for both secondary and higher education. A considerable amount of the vocational training organized by the VDAB and FOREM is carried out at their own training centres, where two types of programme are offered: training for the technical/industrial sectors and training for the service sector.

According to a recent report on training facilities in Belgium, there are some 400 centres with technical/industrial courses in the building, metalworking, electrical, transport, chemical, timber and clothing industries as well as in the hotel and catering industry. Most of these training courses require attendance for thirty-eight hours per week, lasting anything up to a year. The number of participants in technical/industrial training has declined over the past few years, according to the OECD figures, whereas those in the service sector have increased. The latter includes courses such as languages, secretarial training, company administration and management, and information technology. In 1989 there were twenty training centres for the service sector in the French-speaking community catering for over 11,000 people. Just over 4,000 of these were job-seekers, 70 per cent of whom found employment within three months of completing the course. In the Flemish-speaking community there were 33 centres training approximately 31,000 people. According to the latest OECD study, the percentage of job-seekers among the trainees is decreasing steadily.

In addition to the centrally operated regional centres, both FOREM and the VDAB are involved with in-house company training initiatives. The involvement ranges from extending official recognition to in-house training courses to paying out subsidies to company schemes for employees and creating joint training opportunities with industry. The VDAB, for example, has established such joint ventures with the chemical, metalworking and diamond industries.

Managerial and supervisory training

A large percentage of managerial employees, particularly those destined for senior management or technical positions in the larger organizations, are recruited direct from higher education institutions into graduate trainee positions, depending on qualifications and specialization. In the case of university graduates, degree subjects for those entering business tend to have a more directly vocational flavour, although the two-stage process of higher education allows for some switching in midstream. This vocational bias is reflected in the fact that around one-third of all degrees awarded are in science and engineering, the highest proportion in the OECD countries after France (39 per cent).

Training for supervisors and for those selected for internal promotion to higher managerial positions is conducted in approved training centres (either private or one of those run by the regional authorities). The public centres also offer management and business training to craftsmen and the self-employed who run small enterprises. A distinction is drawn between business management and skills training, with 128 hours per year required for each. Most such courses last two years, with some extending to three. A total of 325 courses are provided in fifteen centres in the French-speaking community and twenty-two centres in the Flemish-speaking community.

Figures for 1989 show that in the Flemish-speaking community a total of 15,093 people enrolled for management training and a further 18,194 for specific professional skill courses. In the French-speaking community total enrolments were 8,155 for the same year.

In addition, a variety of commercial companies offer management and business training. However, these are largely unregulated, and standards are best assessed by consultation with local experts.

Training for job-seekers

Training initiatives for job-seekers are broken down into career guidance services, short-term vocational training courses, and individual training within companies. There is also the possibility of financial assistance for collective retraining in companies engaged in restructuring (see below). Those unemployed and in receipt of benefit are eligible to participate in company training schemes, for which they receive an additional payment from the employer on top of their benefit entitlement. This training lasts for a minimum of one month to a maximum of six months, after which the employer is bound to offer a permanent contract of employment.

In Flanders an experimental project was established at the end of 1989 to assist the long-term unemployed back into the labour market: Weer-Werk-Actie (Work Again Action). Since 1991 the programme has been expanded throughout Flanders. The project is aimed at bridging the gap between difficult-to-fill vacancies and the large number of long-term unemployed, through retraining or redirection. According to the VDAB, under whose auspices the project falls, almost 10,000 unemployed people made use of the project in 1991.

French-speaking community initiatives

In the French-speaking community several initiatives have been set up to assist young people and disadvantaged adults into the labour market. The two most noteworthy are the vocational apprenticeship initiatives (*enterprises d'apprentissage professionel*, EAP) and the integrated development programmes (*actions intégrées de développement*, AID).

Unlike other work-training schemes, the EAP is targeted at people aged between 18 and 25 who in some way or other have fallen behind in their education and training, or who are disadvantaged and marginalized. The majority are young people who have exhausted their unemployment benefit entitlement and who do not qualify for other vocational training schemes. EAPs offer vocational training based on work in a simulated company context, and they are run on a strictly non-competitive basis. EAPs are authorized and funded by the French-language community, with some subvention from the European Social Fund. General and vocational training at EAPs lasts up to eighteen months, and concentrates primarily on training in building, carpentry, cattle rearing and small-scale catering. Some thirty-six EAPs have been recognized and in 1990 dealt with about 1,000 young people. The budget for the same year was set at just under BF 30 million (£520,000).

The AID programmes, which have links with the CSC trade union confederation, are in many ways comparable to the EAPs in their target group but are directed at the public sector. At the end of 1991 there were 13 AID projects under way, with over 400 participants. Like the EAPs they receive their funding from the Wallonia regional authorities and from the ESF.

Other training initiatives

A number of training opportunities are provided by and for specific industries: agricultural training, vocational training in the army, training for handicapped workers, training for government ministries and local authorities. In addition to these, there is the widespread use of adult education classes in the evening and at weekends – the Onderwijs voor Sociale Promotie. This is limited to a maximum of twenty-eight hours per week, and covers a comprehensive range of subjects at different levels of qualification.

Subsidies and funding

Funding for vocational training, as for education in general, is largely the responsibility of the regions, following the 1988 constitutional reforms, which devolved increased financial power from central government. According to OECD statistics, Belgium spends around 6 per cent of GDP on education, above the OECD average of 4·8 per cent.

Under the 1991/92 national collective agreement covering all sectors, there is a recommendation that 0·25 per cent of companies' pay bills should be devoted to employment and training initiatives for 'at risk' groups (an increase from 0·18 per cent in 1989/90). Sectoral and company-level collective agreements can increase this percentage and detail specific training measures to be taken. Companies covered by such collective agreements are entitled to an exemption from payment of 0·18 per cent and 0·25 per cent of the wage bill to the sectoral employment fund. 'At risk' groups are defined in the national collective agreement, and include the long-term unemployed, unemployed people with low or no qualifications, young people subject to part-time compulsory education, people re-entering the labour market, the unemployed aged 50 or over, and workers with low qualifications. In cases where no sectoral or company initiative is taken to use the 0·25 per cent for training, an equivalent sum has to be paid into an employment fund (*tewerkstellingsfonds*). Approximately BF 4,500 million (£75·7 million) is raised per year, of which almost 95 per cent is currently channelled direct into company or sectoral training initiatives. However, in the face of concern about the lack of control over precisely how the money is allocated in company and sectoral schemes, and fears that the groups most at risk (notably the long-term unemployed) were less likely to benefit from such programmes, the government decreed in August 1992 that a minimum of 0.10 per cent of the pay bill must be paid into the fund. In addition, companies are to account for the measures they have implemented with the training levy by the end of 1992.

In the metalworking industry, the largest industrial employer with some 240,000 workers, three broad training schemes are operated with funding from the 0·25 per cent programme. The first is targeted at apprentices in the industry, granting subsidies to companies who take on apprentices from among the lower qualified or unemployed. These subsidies vary from BF 50,000 to BF 200,000 (£842–£3,370) per apprentice per year. Secondly, advisers and trainers are provided for a number of regional schemes such as those run by the VDAB for the long-term unemployed (see above). Finally, almost BF 150 million (£2·5 million) is used for in-house company schemes, with responsibility for specific fund allocations given to six joint industry committees.

The various vocational training courses and apprenticeships are financed through a combination of regional subsidies, grants and employer and/or employee levies and contributions. So, for example, the FOREM and VDAB courses receive subsidies from their respective regional authorities, as well as European Social Fund grants, and contributions as levied on companies participating in some of the courses. Part of the collectively agreed wage bill allocations (see above) are channelled into VDAB and FORUM-run courses.

Under certain conditions, new companies, and companies undergoing restructuring in Wallonia, are entitled to a training subsidy from the regional authorities. New companies must prove they are creating at least five new jobs, and companies undergoing restructuring must guarantee no job losses. Subsidies are granted for training of a technical nature only for between four and twenty-six weeks and can go towards the cost of external training or the payment of in-house instructors.

Employee time-off rights

The right to paid educational and training leave (*congé-éducation payé*) is regulated by the Economic Recovery Act, 1985, for employees in the private sector in full-time employment. Public-sector employees and teaching staff are specifically excluded from the legislation. The

Act encourages employees to take courses related to their employment outside working hours. For every fifty minutes of educational activity an employee is entitled to one hour off work, with no loss of salary, up to an annual ceiling of 240 hours for vocational training courses or 160 hours for general education courses. There are concessions on employer social security contributions and partial wage subsidies for time off.

An employee wishing to take training leave must apply in writing with proof of registration on a course. Paid leave is given both for vocational training courses and for more general educational courses recognized by the joint industry committees.

Educational leave is financed through a national educational leave fund to which the state and employers contribute. There are two methods of payment. The first entails contributions to the fund of 0·03 per cent of the total pay bill by employers to cover vocational training: in 1990 the state contributed a total of BF 525 million (£9·05 million) and employers BF 632 million (£10·9 million). Leave for more general education is financed exclusively by the state, and totalled BF 105 million in 1990 (£1·8 million). For 1992 these contribution levels are expected to rise substantially.

The law details the type of educational and training courses qualifying for paid leave. They include vocational training courses of various kinds, evening or weekend higher education courses, study towards university entrance diplomas, industry training courses established by joint industry committees, and courses organized by worker representatives. Educational leave is monitored by works councils (see the third volume in this series, *Industrial Relations*) or by agreement between the employer and the trade union delegation. (The latter is a union-only body set up at company level on the request of one or more unions affiliated to nationally recognized centres.)

The law provides for limits to be placed by the employer on the number of employees entitled to take educational leave at any one time: in companies with fewer than twenty employees the employer can limit leave to a maximum of 10 per cent of the work force at any one time; in companies with twenty to 100 the maximum can be set at 10 per cent of employees 'carrying out the same tasks, as defined by the works council'; in companies with a work force of over 100, educational leave may be covered in a specific collective agreement which effectively removes this issue from the control of the works council.

Appendix 1.1 General educational attainment

Level	Percentage of adult population (1989)
Pre-primary/primary	33
Lower secondary	30
Upper secondary	20
Non-university tertiary	10
University	7

Appendix 1.2 Organizations

National Ministry of Education
Cité administrative de l'Etat
1010 Brussels
tel. + 32 2 564 82 11

VDAB:
Keizerslaan 11
1000 Brussels
tel. + 32 2 506 15 11
fax + 32 2 511 45 43

FOREM:
Boulevard de l'Empereur 5
1000 Brussels
tel. + 32 2 510 20 11

Ministry of Education (Flemish community):
6de verdieping
CAE Arcadengebouw – Blok F
1010 Brussels
tel. + 32 2 210 62 11
fax + 32 2 210 62 23

Ministry of Education (French community):
Rue de la commerce 68A
1040 Brussels
tel. + 32 2 511 72 60
fax + 32 2 511 94 07

Ministry of Education (German community):
Klötzerbahn 32
4700 Eupen
tel. + 32 87 74 40 75
fax + 32 87 74 02 58

Formation professionelle des classes moyennes:
Ministère des classes moyennes
W.C.T. Tour 2
Boulevard Emile Jacqmain 162
1000 Brussels
tel. + 32 2 219 41 50

Chapter 2

Denmark

Denmark has a well developed system of initial and continuing vocational training, with a high level of co-operation between the state, employers and trade unions in the shaping and administration of the system. Legislation introduced in 1991 integrated apprenticeship training and other forms of initial training into a single system combining on-the-job experience with theoretical instruction, and financed by compulsory employer contributions to a training fund.

The education system

Compulsory education lasts nine years (with an optional tenth year) between the ages of 7 and 16. These years are usually spent in a single school known as the *folkeskole*. After completing *folkeskole*, pupils who wish to continue at school may choose between various forms of training and education. The majority of young people continue in either vocational training or upper secondary school.

According to OECD figures, public expenditure on education in Denmark accounted for 6·8 per cent of GDP in 1988 – along with Finland, the highest proportion in the OECD. (It compares with 4·7 per cent in the United Kingdom.)

Lower secondary education

The *folkeskole* is attended by every child for at least seven years. Education at this level may be in municipal schools, in private schools or through home tuition. Municipal schools, which do not charge fees, are by far the most widespread form of basic education, attended by around 90 per cent of Danish children.

Private schools of various kinds take 10 per cent of children at *folkeskole* level. They receive government subsidies of up to 85 per cent of their operating expenses, the balance being made up through the fees charged. Subject to certain conditions, loans can be obtained on favourable terms for the establishment of new private schools. Government subsidies to private education are seen as safeguarding the rights of those who wish their children to receive an alternative education on ideological, political, educational or religious grounds.

The *folkeskole* provide a broad general education in which core academic subjects are combined with instruction in art, music and more practical skills, together with contemporary and vocational studies. There is express emphasis on the ability to form independent judgements and to take and share the responsibility for solving problems.

There is no compulsory examination when young people leave *folkeskole* at 16. On completion, all students are given a leaving certificate stating the subjects they have taken and the marks for their last year's work. Students may, however, choose to sit one of two examinations:

- The Leaving Examination (LE).
- The Advanced Leaving Examination (ALE).

The ALE is available in Danish, maths, English, physics/chemistry and German; the LE, in these five subjects plus Latin, art, woodwork, home economics and typing. Within this framework, pupils may take as many or as few subjects as they wish. The decision on which subjects to study at which level is taken on completion of the seventh year of *folkeskole*.

One alternative to the last three years at *folkeskole* is provided by the *efterskole*, or continuation school. These schools are residential independent schools whose curricula are based mainly on particular political, religious or pedagogical ideas. They are intended as an alternative form of education for young people who do not feel at ease in the usual system, and they tend to place greater emphasis on social and recreational skills and practical work. In 1989–90, around 16,000 pupils attended these types of school, out of a total of 634,000 school pupils.

Upper secondary education

On leaving lower secondary education, students are faced with a number of choices. They can:

- Look for a job.

- Go to folk high school or a specialized boarding school.
- Choose general upper secondary education.
- Opt for vocational training.

About 10 per cent of school leavers choose to quit the education system at this point. The vast majority continue in some form of upper secondary or vocational education.

General upper secondary education. The two most common types of general upper secondary education are three-year courses at a *gymnasium* leading to the Upper Secondary School Leaving Examination (*Studentereksamen*) and two-year courses leading to the Higher Preparatory Examination (*Højere Forberedelseseksamen*, HF).

In addition, it is possible to take the Higher Commercial Examination (*Højere Handelseksamen*, HHX) or the Higher Technical Examination (*Højere Teknisk Eksamen*, HTX), both of which are comparable to the *Studentereksamen* but more vocationally orientated and form the core of technical education (see below).

It is also possible to attend two-year day or evening classes (*studenterkurser*) leading to the *Studentereksamen* or to take all or part of the HF on a single-subject basis.

Admission to *gymnasia* is governed mainly by recommendation from a *folkeskole*. It may be a requirement that students should have achieved satisfactory results in the LE in certain subjects. Students choose either of two main streams – mathematics (sciences) or languages (arts). A common core of subjects is taught at intermediate level, with students choosing at least two subjects from their stream to study at advanced level.

Students who pass the *Studentereksamen* receive a certificate showing their examination grades and the marks for their last year's work. The certificate gives access to university and other types of higher education, although admission to some faculties is granted only to students with a pass in a particular branch of study. Other students may be required to pass supplementary examinations in subjects relevant to their chosen field of study.

The Higher Preparatory Examination (HF) was introduced in 1967 and can be taken by anyone over the age of 18. It confers the right of admission to further education and represents a second route for people with work experience. Since most people cannot pass an examination of this kind without tuition, two-year courses have been set up at *gymnasia*, teacher training colleges and other institutions. There are also three and four-year day and evening classes which enable people to sit the HF on a single-subject basis.

The HF concept has been a great success. Intake has risen from an initial 500 in 1967 to around 12,000 full-time and 48,000 part-time students by the end of the 1980s, with seventy-seven full-time and seventy-nine day and evening courses to choose from.

Whilst traditional *gymnasia* courses are felt to be the natural preparation for tertiary education for 16 year olds, HF courses often cater for somewhat older people who have spent time in commerce or industry. Work experience is taken into account when deciding on admission to HF courses, although most HF students have passed the LE or its equivalent. HF courses have thus become an important type of continuing adult education.

Technical and commercial education: HHX and HTX. Preparation for the HHX takes place at commercial schools. Admission to courses, which normally last for two years, is subject to the completion of basic vocational training (see below) in the field of commerce, clerical work and public administration. There is, however, a parallel one-year course for students who have passed the *Studentereksamen*.

The HTX is taken at technical schools. The course lasts for two years and requires the completion of basic vocational training in one of the main technical fields plus supplementary knowledge of mathematics and physics/chemistry. Passing this examination – combined with other courses at upper secondary level, and/or HF single-subject courses – gives admission to a number of university courses.

HHX and HTX are designed to bridge the gap between basic vocational training and university education. The technical and commercial schools also provide further technical and commercial/administrative courses.

Higher education

Entry to higher and further education requires any of the following qualifications: the *Studentereksamen*, the HF, the HTX or the HHX. However, applicants may be admitted with other recognized qualifications (including foreign ones).

Access to courses is regulated by criteria set by the Ministry of Education for the selection of applicants under legislation introduced in

1977, and quotas are set for each area of study. When fixing the quotas, consideration is given to the estimated future need for graduates, the capacity of the various institutions and the geographical distribution of the applicants.

A co-ordinated clearing system (Koordinerede Tilmelding – the equivalent of UCCA in the UK) permits applicants to apply for admission to more than one institution and thus increase their chances of getting a place.

Applications are screened to check whether they meet the admission requirements. Admission is granted to the institution/course highest on the prospective student's list, provided sufficient places are available. No applicant is offered a place at more than one institution in the final allocation. This system applies only to full-length degree courses – admission to shorter further education courses is arranged by the individual institutions themselves.

The degrees that are awarded follow the common international pattern – a bachelor's (*kandidat*) degree, a master's (*magister*) degree and a doctorate. The *kandidat* degree is usually taken after a minimum of five or six years' study and the *magister* after six to eight years'. However, study may continue for considerably longer, and the student drop-out rate is also relatively high, with 70 per cent of those enrolled completing their degree.

Types of institution. Denmark has three universities (Copenhagen, Aarhus, and Odense), all administered by the Ministry of Education, and two university centres (Roskilde and Aalborg). The latter teach traditional academic subjects, as well as offering more curricular innovation. Aalborg University Centre, opened in 1974, brought together a number of previously independent institutions, including two engineering academies, a school of social work and business economics schools. Aalborg, together with the Technical University of Denmark (located at Lyngby), trains graduate engineers.

There are also a large number of specialized institutions administered by the Ministry of Education which offer advanced and professional education and training in a wide range of occupations. As well as colleges and academies of engineering, which provide shorter (two or three-year) engineering courses leading to the qualification of *teknikum*, there are commercial colleges and single-specialism schools of dentistry, veterinary science, the graphic arts and pharmacy.

The administration of the further education system. Funding for higher education is provided by the state and forms part of the national budget. Higher education expenditure accounts for some 30 per cent of total education spending, above the 20 per cent average for OECD countries (and 19 per cent in the UK).

The administration of universities and other institutions by the Ministry of Education is regulated by the Institutions of Higher Education Act, passed in 1970 and most recently amended in 1989. As well as setting out the institutions' duty to provide instruction and carry out research, the Act obliges the Ministry of Education to lay down regulations for admission, courses, the employment of teachers and research staff, the expulsion of students and the granting of doctorates.

Research normally takes place within the institutions themselves, although many non-university vocationally orientated higher education institutions, such as the branches of the colleges of commerce (*handelshøjskoler*), do not carry out research of their own but make use of results from other institutes of further education. The distribution of research tasks within each institution is decided by a committee.

Teaching staff, students and technical/administrative staff are represented on all the collegiate boards and committees.

Student grants and loans. Financial support runs from August to July, applications being submitted to the institution where the student is enrolled. Support consists of two elements: grants and study loans. Each element is subject to an upper limit, with different rates for students living away from home or with their parents. (Currently, for example, the maximum financial support per month for a student living independently is a DKr 3,000 (£280) grant plus a possible DKr 1,350 (£125) loan. The award of scholarships and grants further depends on the income and circumstances of the student. Before the student's nineteenth birthday the award is also dependent on parental income.

The system of paying grants is fairly flexible. Students are allocated a number of units, each unit representing one month's support, the exact number depending on the duration of the course. Students may then use the units as they wish (rather like using a phonecard), with the proviso that eight units must be used per year. The remaining units may be carried forward for future use: there is no limit on the number of units which may be used per month. This gives students considerable flexibility in arranging their own individual course of study.

Vocational training

Initial vocational training

The first Act of Parliament on the vocational training of young people was the Trade Act of 1857, which abolished, for tradespeople, the necessity of belonging to guilds, which had previously regulated apprentices' conditions. Supervision of apprenticeships was taken over by local tradespeople and business associations, which established evening courses in general and theoretical subjects for apprentices.

The first Apprenticeship Act was passed in 1889, and training was made compulsory for craft trades. The first Trade Committee was set up in the 1920s as a representative body for master craftspeople and trade unions where apprentice training measures could be discussed.

The Apprenticeship Act, 1956, shifted the education and training of apprentices from evening to day classes. The Act provided for the restructuring and modernization of curricula to be supervised by thirty-four joint trade committees – thirty-one for trade and industry and one each for the retail trade, commerce and office work. Under this system, successful completion of an apprenticeship was the basis for the award of a Journeyman's Certificate (*svendebrev*). In the clerical and commercial fields it was sometimes necessary for apprentices to pass examinations on the theoretical side of their training – either the Commercial Assistant's Examination (*handelsmedhjælpereksamen*) or the more comprehensive Commercial Examination (*handelseksamen*).

The joint committees also produced recommendations which, after an experimental period, became the Basic Vocational Training Act (*Erhvervsfaglige grunduddannelser*, EFG) of 1977. The EFG was designed as a parallel to the apprenticeship system, starting with a one-year period of full-time education providing a broad introduction to a number of related trades. After choosing a particular trade, pupils would continue with a combination of theory and practical work along the lines of a traditional apprenticeship.

New legislation which came into effect in January 1991 replaced the 1956 Apprenticeship Act and the 1977 EFG Act and brought basic vocational training and apprenticeship together under a new Basic

Vocational Education and Training Act. The reforms affected the country's fifty-four commercial and fifty-three technical schools and the five schools which offer both technical and commercial subjects. These 112 schools receive about half (48,000) of the typical national year-group of young people.

There are two routes of entry into the system. Trainees can either:

- Begin employment with a company, or
- Start a twenty-week introductory period (corresponding to the first term) at a commercial or technical school.

In both cases there follows a second term of twenty weeks' schooling. Training subsequently alternates between practical work and classroom instruction. Classroom instruction is financed by state grants, with periods of practice being funded in the first instance by the firms involved. Compensation for trainees during the time at school and with the company is financed from the AER (trainee reimbursement fund), which is financed by compulsory employer contributions. The provision of training places is voluntary, and administered by local bodies, the LETC (see below). The two routes are deemed of equal value.

By combining school and practical work, basic vocational education and training aim both to prepare the trainee to take up employment immediately and to provide the basis of further training in the trade and/or participation in continued further education. Great emphasis is therefore laid on relating theory to actual work experience and on flexibility – the ability to adapt to new technology and working practices is highly valued.

The entire process of basic vocational training can take up to five years, alternating between school and work experience, with a maximum of eighty weeks being spent at school. Training for most fields, however, takes three to four years. The previous system comprised around 300 courses. The new legislation has reduced the number to eighty-six, with broad access and late specialization. There is free access, as long as nine years' basic schooling (ten years' in a few cases) has been completed, and there is a free choice of schools.

On completion of initial training, a nationally recognized training certificate is issued (*svendebrev* in the craft trades, *uddannelsesbevis* elsewhere). According to EC comparability standards, this is deemed equivalent, for the engineering industry, to a UK National Vocational Qualification level III or City and Guilds Mechanical Craft Studies 1 and 2. In commerce, where the training period is shorter and the certificate is not based on an apprenticeship-level training, a Danish *uddannelsesbevis* would be equivalent to a UK NVQ level 1–2.

Structure and direction of basic vocational education and training

Technical and commercial schools are self-governing institutions headed by a principal and a governing board, although the ultimate objectives of the vocational education system are governed by law, and the Ministry of Education issues regulations on the objectives and content of courses. Schools are therefore expected to be active in educational and economic planning. There is considerable decentralization to the local representatives of the social partners on the school governing boards and local training committees. Schools are financed by the state via a fixed-subsidy scheme and a legislatively based fixed payment per pupil. Each individual school decides which of the approved types of training it wishes to offer, and there is considerable scope for local experimentation.

Ministry of Education. The central administration of the system is carried out by the Ministry of Education's Department of Vocational Education and Training. Its responsibilities include the approval of new types of training and the drafting of regulations concerning training already offered. The Minister has the power to make binding rulings in these matters, but is required by law to take into account the recommendations of the Vocational Education and Training Council.

Vocational Education and Training Council. The Council is an advisory body whose chair is appointed by the Minister of Education. Of the twenty voting members, eight each are appointed by the DA (the employers' federation) and the LO (the trade union confederation), with one LO member representing the pupils/trainees. The remaining places are filled by members appointed by the Ministers of Labour, Industry and Education and Research, and by local authorities and teachers.

The council's main duties are to submit to the Minister of Education, on its own initiative, recommendations concerning the structure, objectives, content and examination procedures for existing types of training, the inclusion and removal of subjects from the curriculum and qualification requirements for teachers. However, the council also considers all types of general issues that are relevant.

Initiative and co-ordination committees. These may be set up by the council in one or more business sectors and responsibilities may be delegated to them. The main task of the committees is to draw attention to the need for new types of education and training. Their costs are borne by the organizations represented on them.

Trade committees. Trade committees perform a central role as far as curricula are concerned. They are joint employer-union bodies and are responsible for matters relating to the duration, structure, objectives and examination standards of individual types of training.

The regulatory framework – which trade is to provide the core, the ratio between classroom and practical work – is also decided by the trade committees. Additionally, they approve companies as qualified training establishments and rule on conflicts between trainees and companies. The committees and their secretariats are financed by the organizations which form their membership.

School governing boards. School governing boards may consist of six to twelve members. One member each is nominated by the county and municipal councils and the remaining places are filled in equal numbers by employer and labour organizations connected with the district and the vocational areas covered by the school. The board has final managerial responsibility for the school, approves the principal's budget and decides, in association with the principal, which areas of training should be covered to meet the needs of local business. The board employs the principal, who acts as secretary to the board.

Local education and training committees. These are set up and funded by schools for each type of training offered. Committee members are proposed by local branches of employer and union organizations and appointed by the trade committee; by law these must make up a majority of the committee (parity applies). LETCs act in an advisory capacity to schools; they are also required to promote co-operation between schools and local businesses and to find adequate training places in local companies for a school's trainees.

Denmark's system of basic vocational training is well organized and comprehensive, with a long tradition of involvement by the social partners in both policy-making and administration at central and local level on the practical and theoretical sides. Much of the initiative for reform has come from the trade unions and employers themselves, who in turn attach great value to the qualifications awarded by the system.

By the end of the 1980s about 155,000 students were undergoing some kind of basic vocational training: 82,000 EFG students, 43,000 apprentices and around 30,000 choosing basic technical and commercial diplomas. Although figures are not yet available for the new system, it seems likely that intakes will continue at the same level.

Training of vocational school teachers

The training of these teachers is similar to that of *gymnasium* teachers – a period of specialized training and some professional experience form the basis of a course in educational theory and practice. Such courses are offered at the State Institute of Vocational Teacher Training (Statens Erhvervspædagogiske Læreruddannelser). There are also a number of in-service courses for vocational schools. These courses are compulsory for vocational school teachers and must normally be completed within the first two or three years of employment.

Adult education

'Open education'

The Open Education Act came into force in January 1990. Its aim is to give adults the opportunity of further education through vocationally orientated part-time courses and single-subject courses, thus increasing their qualifications for present or future employment.

Courses are offered both at vocational training institutions (technical and commercial colleges) and at centres of further education (universities, business schools, engineering colleges, etc.).

Admission criteria take full account of work experience. No age limit is imposed on open education, and by law the teaching must be organized in such a way that it can be followed outside normal working hours by people in full-time employment. Supplementary legislation secures the right of unemployed people to pursue such courses *during* normal working hours without loss of benefit, subject to proof that it will help their professional prospects.

Participation in open education does not entitle students to receive state financial support, and tuition is not necessarily free. However, the state awards grants to approved open education courses so as to reduce student payments. At present, the grants cover about 80 per cent of operational expenditure, with the balance made up from fees paid by students. Institutions can apportion the grants between various courses as they wish, so that fees on one course can be higher to offset free tuition in others. This makes it possible for courses offered to the unemployed under the new legislation to be free of charge.

Continuing training

The Further Training Act is designed, through government grants, to promote the development of vocationally orientated in-service training and further education to encourage reorganization and innovation in companies. Courses have three main aims:

- The application of new technologies.
- The identification of new market opportunities.
- The improvement of quality and productivity.

They are aimed at non-academic salaried employees and technicians, entrepreneurs and the self-employed.

Activities are planned and implemented locally, to ensure the relevance of the courses. Applicants for grants may be educational institutions, other public institutions or private course organizers. Applications which involve companies are accorded high priority by the authorities. Grants may be given to facilitate the establishment of courses and to reduce the fees payable by participants. Most courses of this type are run at local public education establishments and will have been set up by firms, employers' organizations or trade unions.

Administration is carried out by a council within the Ministry of Education, supported by an advisory group. Subject to courses being approved by the Ministry, there is a basic grant of DKr 20 (£2.15) per lesson for participants registered by companies and DKr 45 (£4.85) for others, plus such discretionary grants as are deemed necessary. The courses do not carry any national qualifications.

In practice, much of the money awarded in grants under this law is spent on research and development work, especially by the vocational schools and universities. This has led in turn to the development of new types of course in the field of adult vocational training – notably the VTP (company-tailored) courses held by vocational schools. The contribution of the Act to vocational education is mainly indirect, in encouraging training institution staff to upgrade their knowledge of technical innovations and export and productivity developments and by making courses more demand-orientated.

Adult vocational training

The vocational training of adult workers was first regulated by the Act on the Training of Unskilled and Semi-skilled Workers (*Specialarbejdereuddannelser*). The Act provided, for the first time, nationwide systematic training for adult workers in all sectors of industry. The curricula of courses were approved by a Training Council, with detailed plans being prepared by a number of Sector Committees. There was equal representation for labour and employers' organizations on both the council and the committees.

The introduction of more complex technology also created a need for further training for skilled workers. This was left in the hands of employers until 1965, when legislation was approved which brought the training of skilled workers (*efteruddannelser for faglærte*) under a system similar to that already established for unskilled and semi-skilled workers.

In 1978 training courses for the long-term unemployed and for young unemployed people (*LAMU kurser* and *EI kurser*) were introduced, administered by municipal authorities and financed by central government.

In 1985 the Adult Vocational Training Act (Arbjedsmarkedsuddanelser, AMU) was passed, combining all the above in a single legislative framework governing all such training for all skill levels.

Training and further training courses for adults are designed to refresh and improve the professional qualifications of workers at all skill levels in the light of technical advances and the requirements of the labour market. Several hundred courses were available in 1991: those aimed at unskilled and semi-skilled workers were completed by around 100,000 people, whilst about 60,000 took part in one or more of the one-to-four-week modular courses designed for skilled workers. The system also arranges job training for work supervisors.

Overall, the AMU costs about DKr 2 billion a year. Half this amount is spent on wage compensation for workers taking the courses. A large part of the expense is met by special funds, the Arbejdsmarkedsuddannelsesfonden (AUD), the Vocational Training Fund, financed by compulsory employee and employer contributions of, for 1990, around DKr 1,300 per month, the balance being made up from public funds. (On average, employees pay around 43 per cent of the levies, and employers 57 per cent.)

The administration of the system is largely devolved to the social partners (see below), with the emphasis on achieving a balance between employer needs for developing skills for immediate application and employee needs for long-term advancement. Courses are short, but culminate in a certificate of completion for the employee.

Structure and direction of the adult vocational training system

The Minister of Labour is the highest administrative authority for the adult vocational training system, and a directorate of the ministry is devoted to this area. The Minister forms a Training Council and appoints its chair. The LO and DA each appoint eight members of the council, and the Ministers of Labour, Education and Industry appoint delegates.

Training committees. The Minister establishes training committees for unskilled and semi-skilled workers' training and one for skilled workers, and appoints a chair for each. The employers' organization, the DA, and the union organization, the LO, each appoint eight members to each of the committees. The brief of the committees is to approve the training programmes and curricula for the courses provided and to make recommendations concerning the distribution of resources.

The actual preparation of the programmes is carried out by a number of Trade Committees. These committees, formed on the initiative of employer and labour organizations, consist of members of those organizations nominated by them (parity applies) and are financed by the organizations themselves. However, the state does provide a subsidy for course preparation in the form of consultant assistance. In addition to planning courses, the committees advise the Training Council on the distribution of grants and training requirements, and monitor the professional content of courses.

Managerial and supervisory training

Managers in Danish industry tend to have engineering qualifications of some type, mainly degrees from a university or one of the eight *teknika* (colleges of engineering), although a qualification in business economics (*cand. merc.*) is also common. Post-entry training depends largely on the size of the company and the level of management. Most such training is done either through in-house training schemes (especially in the case of larger companies) or on courses run by the DA, the employers' federation. The personnel organization IP also provides training and consultancy.

Supervisors, on the other hand, are most often recruited via internal promotion. Their training is often undertaken in-house, or on short courses at local commercial colleges. Such courses confer no recognized supervisory qualification. There is generally little progression from supervisory to management positions.

Appendix 2.1 General educational attainment

Level	Percentage of 25–64 age group
Lower secondary	43
Upper secondary	40
Higher education (non-university)	7
University	10

Source: OECD.

Appendix 2.2 Organizations

Ministry of Labour (International Section):
19 Laksegade
DK-1063 Copenhagen K
Denmark
tel. + 45 33 92 59 00
fax + 45 33 92 55 47

Dansk Arbejdsgiverforening (Danish Employers' Federation):
Vester Voldgade 113
Postboks 386
DK-1503 Copenhagen V
Denmark
tel. + 45 33 93 40 00
fax + 45 33 12 29 76

Landsorganisation i Danmark
(Danish Confederation of Trade
Unions):
Rosenørns Allé 12
DK-1634 Copenhagen V
tel. + 45 31 35 35 41
fax + 45 31 31 79 89

IP (Danish Institute of Personnel
Management):
20 Hauser Plads
DK-1127 Copenhagen
tel. + 45 33 13 15 70
fax + 45 33 32 51 56

Chapter 3

France

Initial vocational training takes place primarily through the state education system, with apprenticeships accounting for a small proportion of trainees, frequently outside mainstream industrial and technical sectors. However, the apprenticeship system was subject to reform in 1992. Continuing training is carried out via the employer, though drawing on external providers.

Tertiary education is structured in two tiers, with state universities providing a general and more arts-orientated education and the elite *grandes écoles* providing more directly professional education – principally in engineering and business studies – for the country's potential top managers and administrators. In addition, there are some specialized technical universities and prestigious business schools with an international reputation and intake, notably INSEAD, located at Fontainbleau.

Training is subject to a number of statutory requirements, including compulsory employer funding, the requirement to establish a company training plan, and time-off rights for employees. The persistence of high unemployment has spurred national training efforts, evidenced in new laws and national collective agreements on training and apprenticeships. High unemployment is also the rationale for the plethora of work experience and insertion courses.

Secondary and tertiary education

Secondary education

School attendance is compulsory until the age of 16. Curricula and staff appointments are highly centralized. The period from the age of 11 to 16 is termed the 'first cycle', takes place in general schools (*collèges*), which are not formally selective, and involves a broad education. In all stages of the system, including much of tertiary education, there is marked emphasis on mathematics. Some secondary school students with academic difficulties may leave the general schools earlier, at 14 or 15, to pursue a preliminary vocational education certificate (CEP) at a technical school (*lycée d'enseignement professionel*, LEP) or take a pre-apprenticeship course.

The 'second cycle' of secondary education entails either further general education, as a preparation for higher education, or a move into initial vocational or technical training. (For initial vocational and technical education in the state system see 'Vocational training' below.)

Education post-16 takes place either in general secondary schools (*lycées*) or in technical secondary schools (*lycées techniques*). In the general secondary schools this cycle culminates after three years in the leaving certificate (*baccalauréat*), with a technical *baccalauréat* option in the technical schools. Technical secondary schools may also train students for a technical certificate (BT), although this is being increasingly supplanted by the technical *baccalauréat*.

The number of school leavers taking the *baccalauréat* has increased rapidly, from 250,000, or 5 per cent of school leavers, in 1950 to an estimated 620,000, or 47·5 per cent of school leavers, in 1992. The government's aim, expressed in its 1989 education reform proposals, is eventually to increase the figure to 80 per cent of school leavers. However, around 13 per cent of school leavers still emerge from the education system without any qualifications (a fall nonetheless from the approximately 25 per cent recorded in 1978). Appendix 3.1 sets out the educational attainment of the labour force in 1991.

The *baccalauréat*, which is considerably broader than the UK A level and regarded as more difficult, entails some specialization, with science options, arts, technology and management variants. It is a prerequisite of access to tertiary education and gives the right of entry into state universities. The crucial *baccalauréat* from the point of view of further advance into a managerial position is 'Bac C', the mathematics and physical sciences option.

Subsequent advance through the education system, and the status of qualifications, are often expressed in terms of years of study after the *baccalauréat* (and written as 'Bac + x' – see below).

Tertiary education

Higher education is notable for the division between the universities and the *grandes écoles*, although the rigidity of the separation has diminished somewhat and there is now scope for interchange, especially at postgraduate level (see below). Managerial recruits from tertiary education come predominantly from the technical specialisms of the universities or from the *grandes écoles*. There is no tradition of recruiting liberal arts graduates into management. On the contrary, great emphasis is placed on the acquisition of quantitative and technical skills, which are regarded as offering the best foundation for the analytical capacity demanded of managers (see also 'Managerial and Supervisory training' below). The main institutions and courses are as follows.

Technical studies. Technical universities (*instituts universitaires de technologie*, IUTs), established in 1969 in response to the need for less protracted technical education, offer two and three-year courses located mid-way between the *baccalauréat,* and longer university courses. There are around seventy of these technical universities, with a total of some 62,000 students. Entrance to IUTs is selective, based on school reports.

The qualifications offered by the technical universities, rated as 'Bac + 2', include the university diploma of technology (*Diplôme universitaire de technologie*, DUT). The acquisition of a DUT diploma may lead on to further studies at one of the state universities. Technical sections of *lycées* also offer technical training, leading to the higher technical certificate (*Brevet de technician supérieur*, BTS). (According to the UK National Institute of Economic Research, this is a 'higher intermediate qualification' and rated as equivalent to HND or HNC in the UK.)

Universities. Universities, of which there are over seventy, are state-run and have a non-selective admission policy as long as students have obtained the school leaving certificate, the *baccalauréat*. This has led to a high drop-out rate after the first-year exams, with only about 50 per cent of new admissions actually graduating. One exception to the rule is the University of Paris Dauphine, which concentrates on management courses and operates an effective selection policy.

There are currently around a million students enrolled in the state universities. University courses are divided into three 'cycles', each cycle lasting around two years. The first two-year cycle is a general preparatory study course in a variety of subjects, leading to a general university studies diploma, the DEUG (*Diplôme d'études universi-*

taires générales) or the more vocationally relevant DEUST (*Diplôme d'études universitaires scientifiques et techniques*). Both would be classified as Bac + 2.

The second cycle is more specialized and can lead to a variety of qualifications, depending on the subjects studied. A qualification taken after one year of this cycle confers the *licence*, or bachelor's degree (Bac + 3). Two years of study culminate in the *maîtrise*, or master's degree (Bac + 4), the most common university qualification. Vocationally relevant examples include the MST (*Maîtrise des sciences et techniques*), the management science degree, MSG (*Maîtrise de sciences de gestion*) or the information sciences degree, MIAGE (*Maîtrise de méthodes informatiques appliquées à la gestion*). There is also a three-year second-cycle qualification in engineering, the *magistère*, which requires both academic work and a practical spell in industry (*Stage*).

The third cycle is for postgraduate work, leading either to a diploma in higher specialist studies (the DESS, *Diplôme d'études supérieures specialisées*) or the DEA (*Diplôme d'études approfondies*). Both are conferred after one year's third-cycle study. The DEA also typically leads on to research and study for a doctorate.

Grandes écoles. The *grandes écoles* are a unique feature of the French system of higher education and management training, and represent the apotheosis of its technical and quantitative bias. Founded in the nineteenth century, originally for the education of the country's military elite, *grandes écoles* now train the country's top administrators and politicians. Most of the top managers in French industry have also been educated at a *grande école*. Whilst some *grandes écoles* are run directly by the national Ministry of Education, and in the case of the Ecole Polytechnique by the Defence Ministry, others are operated by local chambers of commerce or are private. There are thought to be about *160 grandes écoles* in all.

Among the best known *grandes écoles* are the Ecole Polytechnique, known as 'X', and the Ecole Nationale d'Administration, ENA, both of which confer engineering diplomas. In the area of business administration the three Paris-based *grandes écoles* are the Ecole des Hautes Etudes Commerciales (HEC), the Ecole Supérieure des Sciences Economiques et Commerciales (ESSEC) and the Ecole Supérieure de Commerce de Paris (ESCP). The Ecole Supérieure de Commerce in Lyon is the leading provincial business school. However, there are also many smaller local *écoles*, and applicants may apply for several and accept the offer of the most highly regarded.

The *grandes écoles* are highly selective, and entrance to them is gained only through a stiff entrance exam. Students prepare for it by undertaking two years of preparatory studies in *classes préparatoires*, organized by the *lycées*, following acquisition of the *baccalauréat*.

Courses are for three years and lead to a diploma (usually rated as Bac + 5 because of the period of preparation prior to entry). *Grandes écoles* specializing in business administration may also offer supplementary MBA courses. Most *grandes écoles'* courses include at least one placement (*Stage*), and in some business schools students are encouraged to offer consultancy expertise to companies. As a rule the *grandes écoles* do not offer postgraduate education, as the diploma (or equivalent qualification) is regarded as a sufficient and easily understood high-level qualification for prospective employers.

Vocational training

A distinction is drawn between intial training, the bulk of which takes place in state educational institutions, and continuing or supplementary training, which is organized via employers. Apprenticeships are still of less importance than the state system in providing initial training, although recent reforms are intended to bolster this form of training (see below).

Whilst the education system classifies qualifications in terms of years after the *baccalauréat*, the vocational training system has its own hierarchy, beginning with level V (for skilled workers with an initial vocational training qualification) and rising to levels I and II (for managers and engineers with at least Bac + 4).

Initial vocational training: the state system

Most initial vocational training follows the end of compulsory education at 16. However, as noted above, some school students (about 10 per cent) may leave secondary school at 14 or 15, go on to a vocational training school (*lycée d'enseignement professionel*) and begin working towards one of the recognized initial vocational qualifications, the CAP or BEP (see below). A further quarter of the age group move on to these schools at the age of 16 and pursue the same qualifications.

The principal initial vocational qualification is the vocational training certificate (*Certificat d'aptitude professionelle*, CAP) which takes three years to acquire, and entails practical and theoretical training. (Young people who leave school without any qualification are often those who have had difficulty with the theoretical parts of the CAP.) The less specialized vocational studies certificate (*Brevet d'études professionelles*, BEP) takes two years, with qualifications primarily for occupations in the service sector. Both would be regarded as initial qualifications for a skilled or semi-skilled worker. (In a comparative study carried out by the UK NIESR the CAP/BEP qualifications were rated as equivalent to a City and Guilds Part II pass – see 'Further reading'.)

A higher degree of technical education is provided initially in specialized *lycées*. As noted above, it may be for either a technical or a vocational *baccalauréat* or for the technician certificate (*Brevet de technicien*, BT). According to the NIESR study referred to above, this level of qualification was deemed 'lower intermediate', and rated as equivalent to a BTEC National Certificate and National Diploma.

Apprenticeship

There is a recognized system of apprenticeship, accounting for training primarily in craft occupations in small enterprises. The system was overhauled in 1992 through a national collective agreement and corresponding legislation. Part of the reason lay in the continuing high level of unemployment, some criticism of the usefulness of the state-provided CAP qualification, and the stagnating number of apprenticeships (at around 230,000 in all, compared with the approximately 1·3 million in vocational and technical secondary schools). Apprenticeships had also acquired the image of providing a source of cheap temporary labour, with many firms failing to offer apprentices a job on qualifying. In public discussion it was emphasized that the best direction in which to move would be towards the comprehensive German 'dual system', built on the apprenticeship relationship and based on experience of employment as well as theoretical training.

The national collective agreement of 8 January 1992 increased pay for apprentices, expressed as a percentage of the statutory national minimum wage, the SMIC. The agreement also increased flexibility regarding the length of apprenticeship contracts and the content of courses, which is determined at branch level, and increased the amount of information available to prospective apprentices. The main provisions of the agreement were incorporated into a law on apprenticeship passed on 17 July 1992.

Apprenticeship is defined in the Labour Code as 'a means of affording to young people . . . general theoretical and practical training leading to a vocational qualification'. The training may be carried out partly on company premises and partly at an apprentice training centre (*centre de formation d'apprentis*, CFA). All apprenticeships must be registered at a CFA. Apprenticeship training is financed by the apprenticeship training tax, totalling 0.6 per cent of the pay bill and payable by all employers. (The bulk of the revenue raised from the tax actually goes to finance other training and educational institutions, including higher education.)

Apprentices must be aged 16–25 at the beginning of the contract, which must be in writing and registered with the relevant labour authorities. The length of the contract must be at least equal to the length of the course to be undertaken, and is customarily one to three years. Around 70 per cent of contracts are for two years, although in 1991 14 per cent were for one year only. Contracts may be extended in the case of failed examinations, if the apprentice is handicapped, or by special derogation (for example, in the case of military service).

Apprenticeship training contracts generally lead to recognized vocational qualifications such as the basic CAP, the BT and BEP, or in some cases to more advanced qualifications such as the BTS and DUT technical qualifications (see above).

Duties of the employer. An employer who takes on trainees on an apprenticeship contract must register them with an Apprentice Training Centre (CFA). The employer must ensure that the apprentice receives the appropriate practical experience within the company and that the experience progresses in line with the theoretical training. Training may be carried out jointly at the workplace and at the training centre. The employer must also oversee the apprentice's entry for a vocational training diploma, and consult the works committee on apprentice training. Time spent by the apprentice on theoretical training is counted as working time. Apprentices enjoy the same employment protection as that offered to permanent employees.

Payment of apprentices. Apprentices are paid a percentage of the national minimum wage, the SMIC, which varies from 30 per cent (for a 16–17 year old in the first year of training) to 80 per cent (for a 21+ year old in the second year). These rates represent a substantial increase over the pre-1992 percentages as a result of the new apprenticeship law. In August 1992 the SMIC stood at FF 5,756·14 (£592) per month. This is the legal minimum rate and may be improved upon by collective agreement. The payment is made by the employer, who may be able to claim back salary paid for time spent in theoretical training at training centres from a national fund (*Fonds national interconsulaire de compensation*) if the employer is a contributing member.

Employers are exempt from some social charges for apprentices for the duration of their contract.

Apprenticeship contracts terminate at the agreed date, although the contract may be ended by either party within two months of commencement without any reason needing to be given. When the contract has expired the apprentice may be taken on by the company in question. If not, the apprentice may continue in training by means of a further apprenticeship contract or may claim unemployment benefit.

The vast majority (around 70 per cent) of apprentices undertake to train for a qualification relevant to a specific industry. The number of apprentices grew rapidly in the years 1987–9, following overhaul of the system. There was a slight reduction in 1990 but the number of apprenticeship contracts increased by 600 in 1991, bringing the new yearly total to 131,797. Some 70 per cent of apprentices begin their apprenticeship directly on leaving school. Just under a third are female, compared with 23 per cent in 1976.

Initial vocational training for the unemployed: sandwich courses

A number of schemes exist to encourage firms to take on and train the unemployed, many of whom obtained no vocational qualifications at school or lack work experience. For those people not in employment a range of training courses are provided under the heading *formation en alternance* or sandwich courses. Such courses are usually governed by a fixed-term contract and are designed to combine theoretical instruction with practical training, on the job. Originally devised for young people under 26, this type of training contract has since been extended to the long-term unemployed. Employers are offered a range of incentives, such as exemption from social security contributions, state financial aid and exemption from the obligation to count such employees as part of the company's registered work force. A total of 200,000 people benefited from the courses in 1991 and the government hoped to increase the figure to 400,000 over the next five years. The main types of sandwich training contracts and work experience contracts are as follows.

Qualification contract (contrat de qualification). Available to young people of 16–25 years who have gained no academic qualification or who do not possess sufficient qualifications to find employment. It is based on a mixture of training and practical work experience, training having to account for at least a quarter of the contracted period. The contract is for a fixed term, usually between six months and two years. Training is carried out at a public education centre or a public or private training organization. The company must have an agreement with the relevant training centre, or have concluded a framework agreement with the state and an industry or multi-industry association, before offering qualification contracts. The trainee receives a salary calculated as a proportion of the statutory national minimum wage, the SMIC, depending on age and length of contract, paid by the company. Companies are exempt from social charges for these employees.

Return-to-work contract (contrat de retour à l'emploi). Designed to help the long-term unemployed and people with disabilities to gain work experience and marketable skills. Contracts can be fixed-term or permanent, but if fixed-term must last for six to eighteen months. Employment may be part-time, but must run to at least twenty-four hours a week, including training. Salary is paid by the employer, who benefits from a number of incentives, including a lump sum of FF 10,000 (£1,050) for each full-time employee taken on, reimbursement of training costs, exemption from employers' social charges for the employees concerned, and exclusion of these employees from the company's register of employees.

Solidarity contract (contrat emploi-solidarité). Designed for young people aged 16–25 with some technical qualifications, the unemployed aged 50 and over, those who have been unemployed for twelve months or more and those who receive the state minimum monthly restart income, the RMI. These contracts are fixed-term and part-time (20 hours weekly), concluded for a minimum of three months and a maximum of twelve months. They can be renewed twice within the maximum duration limit, which may be extended to twenty-four months. Persons employed on these contracts are paid at the rate of the national minimum wage, the SMIC. This rate is financed up to 85 per cent by the state (100 per cent in some cases); the state will also pay part of or all training costs up to a 400 hour limit.

'Orientation' contracts (*contrats d'orientation*), established by legislation passed in December 1991, replace a previous type of work experience scheme, the SIVP (*stage d'initiation à la vie professionnelle*), which was similar but renewable and regarded as prone to abuse. The new contracts are fixed-term, lasting between three and six months, non-renewable and available to young people experiencing difficulty in finding work and aged under 23 years, or 26 years in exceptional cases. They are paid, at a rate varying between 30 per cent and 65 per cent of the national minimum wage, by the employer, who is exempt from social charges for such employees during the period of the contract.

Training in the public sector

Like private-sector employees, people employed in the public sector have access to training in two main ways: through training plans devised by the employing organization, or by taking training leave which is nationally administered and financed by special funds (see above).

A framework agreement on training in the civil service was signed by the social partners concerned in June 1989. The agreement provided for a minimum of 2 per cent of the wage bill to be spent on training measures. This target has been attained, although it is generally accepted that the average amount spent on training in the private sector is 3·2 per cent of the wage bill. A total of 1·85 million civil servants received some form of training in each year of the three-year agreement, although the spread was reported to be uneven as between Ministries.

A new agreement was signed on 7 July 1992 with the aim of ensuring the continuation of training provision over the next three years and raising the minimum amount spent on it to 3·2 per cent of the wage bill. Employees continue to be entitled to a minimum of three or four days' training per year, depending on their status. The agreement increases remuneration for employees on training leave and provides 100 per cent of pay for those on training leave necessitated by departmental restructuring (*congé de restructuration*).

Training initiatives at industry level

Training arrangements have recently been incorporated into a number of industry collective agreements, reflecting the higher profile which training has acquired. One example is the new national agreement in the insurance industry, signed in May 1992 and covering 95,000 employees nationally. Under the agreement, employees without the school leaving certificate, the *baccalauréat*, or an equivalent technical qualification, and with three years' continuous service are allocated training 'capital' of 400 hours. It may be used on different training programmes, and employees may transfer unused portions of their 'capital' to other companies in the industry should they change their job.

Expenses incurred under the scheme may be included in the statutory required expenditure on training (1·5 per cent of the pay bill – see below), but the scheme must not replace any existing company training scheme or the right to individual employee training (*congé individuel* – see below). The measure will be reviewed after a period of five years. The agreement also increased the minimum amount to be spent on training to 2 per cent of the wage bill from January 1993.

The incorporation of a clause in an industry agreement obliging companies to spend 2 or 3 per cent of the wage bill on training is quite common. This commitment is considerably higher than the statutory minimum of 1·4 per cent, although the average amount spent by companies on training is thought to be around 3·1 per cent.

During 1992 employers and unions in the metalworking industry also reviewed training arrangements, the negotiations concluding with an agreement to improve access to training and widen recognition of qualifications.

Countering the shortage of engineers

In the late 1980s it became apparent that France, like some other Western European countries, faced a shortage of engineers. Engineering colleges were training around 14,000 a year whilst demand was growing steadily. In 1989 there were some 400,000 qualified engineers working in France, and it was estimated that the country would need twice that number in twenty years' time. One of the main problems of increasing the supply was seen to be the average length of training, five years.

In September 1990 the Engineering Qualifications Commission

(*Commission des titres d'ingénieurs*) oversaw the setting up of a variety of training schemes designed to help technical staff (holders of DUT or BTS qualifications) with five years' experience gain engineering diplomas through a mixture of theoretical and practical training. By September 1991 some thirty different schemes in a variety of educational establishments were training over 1,800 technicians to gain professional engineering qualifications, mainly in electronics, computing, mechanical engineering, construction and agriculture.

Managerial and supervisory training

The ranks of supervisor (*agent de maîtrise*) and manager (*cadre*) enjoy legal recognition in France, and their status is defined in collective agreements. There is a recognized qualification for supervisors which is validated by the relevant trade associations in collaboration with ANFOPPE (Association nationale pour la formation et le perfectionnement du personnel d'entreprise). Whereas first-line managers and lower-level cadres will typically be included in industry job classification schemes, with their grade often defined in terms of the formal qualifications they possess, senior managers will be outside such classification schemes but are often dealt with in industry agreements. Access to the status of *cadre* may be by internal promotion, with the acquisition of appropriate formal technical qualifications and several years' experience, or following recruitment as a graduate and some experience, depending on the employee's higher education qualification. A *grande école* graduate would usually be classified as a *cadre* from the outset: an employee with a basic technical education would need to clock up several years' experience. Entry to the ranks of the most senior management is overwhelmingly via higher education and the possession of a university, or *grande école*, diploma. In general, managers are more highly educated than their British counterparts, and around 40 per cent have qualifications rated as Bac + 4–5 (that is, either a university *maîtrise* or a *grande école* diploma).

However, practice is likely to differ between small and large companies, the former tending to train managers with technical qualifications on the job rather than attempting to recruit *grande école* graduates, whose ultimate destination is likely to be a large organization.

According to a 1990 survey carried out by the magazine *l'Etudiant*, out of a total of 108 chief executives of large companies, sixty-five had been educated at the four top *grande écoles* (Polytechnique, ENA, HEC and IEP), with thirty-one trained at the Polytechnique alone. Only four were educated at state universities, and one had risen through the ranks (a so-called *autodidacte*). A small number of CEOs followed *grande école* education with either an MBA or a spell at an Ivy League university in the United States. A slightly larger number had attended two *grandes écoles*, completing their education at a more specialized institution.

The bias towards recruiting the products of *grandes écoles* can also be seen in the graduate intake of the major companies included in the *Etudiant* graduate recruitment guide, where universities (whose students outnumber *grandes écoles* students by a ratio of 10 : 1) often account for 10 per cent or less of intended new managerial recruits.

Qualifications gained at the *grandes écoles* broadly follow the same format as those conferred by universities and include:

- Engineering degrees and diplomas of higher business education.
- The *maîtrise* and, more rarely, a doctoral qualification.
- A *diplôme de mastère*, broadly equivalent to the US MBA qualification.

MBAs are offered by some private business schools, but are not generally considered essential as a management training qualification by recruiting companies. MBAs tend to be favoured by consultancies and the staff of business schools. According to one recent study (see Barsoux and Lawrence, under 'Further Reading'), two-thirds of staff time at INSEAD, originally established to provide MBA courses, is now spent on short courses for existing managers.

Most higher education qualifications involve a period of practical experience in industry or commerce, and male graduates will also have undergone a period of compulsory military service.

Although the 1980s saw a broadening of managerial training style and content, with greater emphasis on interpersonal and overall management skills to supplement the analytical capacity fostered in the *grandes écoles*, there is still concern about the narrow social base and heavily theoretical training of French managers.

Consultation on training

There are obligations on employers at both sectoral level, through collective agreements, and at enterprise level, where they must prepare a training plan (*plan de formation*) and consult their works councils.

Industry level

It is obligatory for negotiations to take place at industry level every five years between the relevant unions and employer organizations. The topics covered by the negotiations were widened under the training law of 31 December 1991 (No. 91-1405). Negotiations must cover the following main areas:

- The type of training schemes in operation or preparation.
- Recognition of the qualifications obtained by this training.
- The position of young people in the company with regard to vocational training.
- The training needs of those with few or no qualifications or skills.
- Equality for men and women with regard to training.
- The particular training problems encountered by companies with fewer than ten employees.
- How companies can give practical effect to provisions agreed at branch level.

A date for the next consultation meeting must be arranged at the end of the meeting.

Company level

Companies bound by a sectoral collective agreement should have a programme of several discussions a year (*un programme pluriannuel*) to outline the kind of training made available by the company and the way in which it is being used. Meetings should take into account:

- Economic factors.
- Investment levels.
- Technology.
- Work organization.
- Working time within the company.

The social partners' agreement on training of 3 July 1991 recommends that such meetings should be held three times a year.

Almost 30 per cent of all company agreements in 1991 were to do with training, predominantly in the metalworking and banking sectors, according to the Ministry of Labour's annual collective bargaining report.

The training plan. Under the Labour Code (articles L.932-6) the employer must draw up a training plan (*plan de formation*) each year in consultation with the works committee or, in establishments with under fifty employees, with staff representatives (see *Industrial Relations* in this series). The plan should contain details of existing training schemes within the company and schemes proposed for the coming year. The plan is to be drawn up in conjunction with the obligations upon employers to consult employee representatives annually on training (see below). According to a report on training in France published by the UK National Economic Development Office, training plans were seen as a useful means of dialogue by companies but regarded by training organizations as rarely matching the expectations raised and often 'very basic' (NEDO, *The Making of Managers*; see 'Further Reading').

Informing and consulting works councils. There is an obligation to consult works councils (or staff representatives in smaller firms) on the implementation of the training plan, and on proposals for the coming year. Works councils or staff representatives must be informed two or three times a year, depending on the size of the company, of the number of employees on sandwich course training contracts (see above). They must also be kept up to date on the facilities available for young people on training contracts and for tutors and trainers. Works councils must be consulted on the facilities available to people on work experience programmes which form a compulsory part of training for professional diplomas.

Continuing vocational training

Continuing vocational training (*formation professionelle continue*) is available to all employees by law, with the aim of adapting skills to technological change and maintaining or improving on existing skills. Company training programmes must be set out in a formal training plan, and there are statutory requirements on the minimum level of expenditure. In all, around 5 million workers are thought to benefit from some form of training each year, a quarter of the work force.

Legislative framework

Continuing training is regulated by legislation passed in December 1991 (law No. 91-1405), which incorporated the provisions of a national collective agreement concluded in July 1991, replacing a 1970 agreement. The main aim was to increase the funding of training and to raise awareness of training opportunities at sectoral level. All firms are required to meet the minimum levels of training expenditure or pay a levy to training funds: the levy was increased from 1·2 per cent of the wage bill to 1·4 per cent in 1992 and to 1·5 per cent on 1 January 1993. Of this total, 0·3 per cent of the pay bill must be for training young workers and 0·2 per cent is to pay for the training of employees on training leave (see below). It does not cover introductory on-the-job training. Companies with fewer than ten employees pay 0·15 per cent of the wage bill (see also below).

Training can be carried out within the company or at a variety of public and private training institutions. The main public institutions are:

- Those under the supervision of the Ministry of National Education, such as the 5,000 *lycées* and public colleges offering courses.
- Technical universities.
- Engineering schools and universities.
- The national centre for correspondence course education, CNED.

The tripartite national adult training association (Association nationale pour la formation professionelle des adultes) is overseen by the Ministry of Labour and Vocational Training: it employs 5,000 tutors in 175 training centres.

Training is also provided by private organizations, including chambers of commerce, which must be registered with the state. There are around 200 training organizations created and administered by industry and multi-industry bodies which organize work placements, particularly in small and medium-sized companies. Similarly, work placements may be organized by a variety of non-profit-making organizations, such as trade unions. In addition, a number of profit-making organizations, such as language training companies or management training organizations, organize a variety of courses.

The Vocational Training Federation (Fédération de la formation professionelle, FFP) was created in June 1991, and encompasses three large private national organizations offering vocational training and advice, Union nationale des organismes privés de formation continue (see Appendix), Syntec formation and Chambre syndicale nationale des organismes de formation. Together these organizations represent some 300 private training organizations which have agreed to be bound by a code of conduct and to maintain minimum quality standards.

Employee time-off rights

Continuing vocational training is governed by the Labour Code (art. L900-1), the provisions of which may be improved upon by collective or company agreement. By law, all employees are entitled to continuing vocational training. This may take a variety of forms. One of the most common is individual training leave (*congé individuel de formation*), which is paid absence of up to one year for full-time training or 1,200 hours for part-time training outside the company. In order to qualify for such leave, employees must have at least twenty-four months' non-consecutive general work experience and twelve months' employment with their current employer.

Employers may refuse to grant or may decide to defer leave if the number of employees absent would exceed 2 per cent of the work force. Employees who have already been on individual training leave may not request a further period of training leave within certain time limits, depending on the length of leave already taken. Employees must notify their employer of a request to take training leave within thirty days for leave of up to six months or for part-time training, and within sixty days for leave of more than six months. The employer has ten days in which to accept or refuse the employee's request. Reasons must be given for a refusal.

An employee on vocational training leave, who is entitled to full pay for a period, is remunerated by payments from vocational training organizations, which in turn are financed by statutory annual company payments (see below).

The take-up of training leave has remained fairly low, and employers in small companies – according to the NEDO study (see above) – appear hostile to the idea and loathe to publicize opportunities. In addition, it has been suggested that small and medium-sized companies would rather simply pay the compulsory levy than give employees transferable skills which could see them recruited by larger firms. Some 26,000 requests were granted in 1990, a fall from the approximately 45,000 per year in the mid-1980s.

Financing

Vocational training is financed principally by companies, with the state and regional authorities also providing some funding. A proportion of finance is raised by levies on firms, some of which are paid in any event (the apprentice training tax – 0·6 per cent of the pay bill) whilst others are payable only if the firm spends less than the legally prescribed total. Some FF 57 billion (£5·9 billion) is devoted to the financing of continuing training each year in all, accounting for around 1·4 per cent of GDP.

Legal requirements

Since 1971 there has been a statutory obligation for all companies to devote a certain sum to staff training. In companies with under ten employees a sum equivalent to 0·15 per cent of the total wage bill must be made available; in companies of ten or more employees this sum is 1·5 per cent of the wage bill. Of this, 0·3 per cent of the pay bill must be devoted to the training of young workers or paid to the Exchequer and 0·2 per cent must be paid to external training centres offering courses to employees on individual training leave (*congé individuel de formation* – see above). The rest of the money may be used in a variety of different ways: financing the training activities of the company's own staff; financing centres for the training of the unemployed or other training centres; financing a central training fund, *fonds d'assurance formation*; or financing retraining (or *conversion*) contracts, which by law must be offered to all workers made redundant.

The company must submit an estimate of its prospective pay bill for the coming financial year, with pay growth accounted for by an estimate included in the finance bill each year, together with allowable training expenses. The return goes to the tax authorities, who are responsible for the monitoring and enforcement of levies/training expenditure.

Investment in training

According to a study carried out by the training research organization Cereq (Centre d'études et de recherche sur les qualifications), companies spent an average of 3·1 per cent of the wage bill on training in 1990, financing a total of 140 million training hours for 2·9 million employees.

This average figure naturally varies according to company size and sector, with larger companies investing more in training than smaller, owner-managed companies. An average of 7·9 per cent of employees in companies with ten to nineteen staff had received some kind of training, whereas the average was 52·9 per cent in companies with 2,000 or more employees. Similarly, average hours spent in training totalled thirty-eight in small companies, compared with fifty-four in companies with over 2,000 employees.

Investment in training also varies according to industry, with commercial aviation spending the highest amount on training (13 per cent of the wage bill) and consumer goods, metalworking and construction spending under 2 per cent of the wage bill. According to the study, men are more likely to receive training than women, with eighty-two women trained for every 100 men, although this is an improvement on the figure of sixty-nine to 100 recorded in 1982. Those with high-profile jobs are more likely to receive training: 52 per cent of technicians and supervisors and 49 per cent of engineers, compared with 29 per cent of white-collar workers and 25 per cent of blue-collar workers. Vocational training appears to be most often used as a means of enhancing employee skills for those who are comparatively highly qualified, rather than offering a means for less qualified employees to gain new skills and embark upon a change of career direction.

The state contributes around FF 19 billion annually to training. It finances schemes for the unemployed and the young unemployed, the disadvantaged and minority groups, and general information on the types of schemes available. Local authorities spend an annual FF 4 billion on training, mainly on the formulation of training and apprenticeship policy in their local area.

Tax credits for training (*crédits d'impôt formation*)

The 1988 budget introduced the notion of tax credits for companies whose expenditure on training is over and above basic legal requirements. The credit, initially for the years 1988–90, was equal to 25 per cent of the excess training expenditure of the company, up to a ceiling of FF 1 million. This provision was renewed on a temporary basis for the period 1991–3. All companies offering training to their employees are eligible, irrespective of their sector of activity, number of employees or status.

In the case of training for unskilled employees or those with a low level of skills, employees of 45 years or over, and any training expenditure of companies with fewer than fifty employees, tax credits are equal to 40 per cent of expenditure.

Appendix 3.1 Qualifications of the work force

Qualification	Percentage of work force (1991) 25–39 year olds	All
In initial education	0·9	1·2
Basic school leaving certificate (CEP)	25·3	34·0
BEPC	7·5	6·7
CAP, BEP (initial training)	32·8	29·2
Baccalauréat, Brevet professionel	11·3	9·6
Bac + 2, BTS, DUT	10·7	8·1
Bac + 4 or 5 or *grande école* diploma	8·6	8·0
Not stated	3·0	3·2

Source: OECD.

Appendix 3.2 Organizations

Ministry of Labour and Vocational Training:
127 rue de Grenelle
75700 Paris
tel. + 33 1 40 56 60 00
fax + 33 1 40 56 67 44

Conseil national du patronat français (CNPF) (national employers' organization):
31 rue Pierre Ier de Serbie
75016 Paris
tel. + 33 1 40 69 44 44

Association nationale pour la formation professionelle des adults (National Adult Vocational Training Association):
13 place du Générale de Gaulle
93108 Montreuil-sur-Bois Cedex
tel. + 33 1 48 70 50 00
fax + 33 1 48 58 34 32

Centre d'études et de recherche sur
les qualifications (CEREQ):
9 rue Sextius Michel
75015 Paris
tel. + 33 1 45 75 62 63

Union nationale des organismes
privés de formation continue
297 rue de Vaugirard
75015 Paris
tel. + 33 1 48 56 18 00

Centre pour le développement de
l'information sur la formation
permanente (National Training
Information Centre):
Tour Europe Cedex 07
92049 Paris La Défense
tel. + 33 1 47 78 13 50
fax + 33 1 47 73 74 20

Chapter 4

Germany

The outstanding feature of education and training in Germany is the 'dual system' of initial vocational training, with its implied commitment to broad-based skills for all and investment in people across the range of academic ability. The dual system is seen as the foundation of a high-skill economy and as an important element in social integration. Although the German system has its internal and external critics, it continues to demonstrate great strengths and has been looked on as a model by those eager to match German industrial performance. However, the dual system is deeply rooted in a strong tradition of guilds and local self-regulation as well as in a dense network of tripartite institutions not easily transplanted elsewhere.

High levels of training for skilled workers are reinforced by recognized further training in intermediate skills, tied into the dual system and creating a substantial reservoir of technically and practically trained employees with managerial potential.

Vocational training in Germany is underpinned by financial and institutional support from the public employment service (see below), with grants and loans to help both employers and employees.

The education system

The system of education and many aspects of vocational training are the responsibility of the constituent *Länder* (states) of the Federal Republic. At primary or secondary level there may be differences between the *Länder*, with a more traditional curriculum in Bavaria and a more 'progressive' approach in central and northern Germany, where the Social Democrats have held power longer. The vast majority of children, around 95 per cent, go to schools in the state system. As the section on secondary education below illustrates, this is attributed not only to the general quality of schooling but also to the fact that the system embodies a large measure of selection, giving little incentive to look to the private sector in search of a traditional academic orientation.

Compulsory education begins in the year in which children complete their sixth year, and continues for nine or ten years, depending on the *Land*. The transition from primary to secondary school may take place either from the fifth or from the sixth year, again depending on the *Land*. However, young people who leave school at 15 are required by law to continue in some form of education (maybe as part of initial vocational training) until the age of 18.

Secondary education

There is selection at the transition to secondary education, based on examination results and teacher assessment. In most *Länder* there are three types of secondary school:

- The *Gymnasium*, which takes the more academically gifted.
- The *Realschule*, which offers intermediate-level secondary education, most of its pupils going directly into vocational training after obtaining a school leaving certificate (the *Mittlere Reife*).
- The *Hauptschule*, which takes lower-ability pupils, most of whom leave at 15 and can undertake a preparatory course prior to entering initial vocational training, the *Berufsgrundbildungsjahr*.

In some *Länder*, notably in Berlin, comprehensive schools (*Gesamtschulen*) have been established. They tend to exist alongside the other types of school rather than to displace them, and so have rarely proved truly comprehensive, given the attractions of the *Gymnasium*. Approximately 30 per cent of pupils are in *Gymnasien*, 30 per cent in *Realschulen*, 35 per cent in *Hauptschulen* and 6 per cent in comprehensive schools.

In the first instance, only an education at a *Gymnasium* confers a qualification which gives the right to enter a university. This is the *Abitur* exam, which is taken by around a quarter of all school students, typically at the age of 19. The syllabus is both rigorous and broad. Most pupils take two core subjects but must, in addition, study a foreign language and either maths or a physical science, as well as other subjects. The final mark, which may influence university entrance, is based both on examination results and on progress during the course.

However, there are other routes, via vocational training plus supplementary study, which offer access to tertiary education. Determining what qualifications and study can be regarded as equivalent to the *Abitur* is a matter for the individual *Länder*.

Higher education

There are two basic types of higher education institution: full universities (which may be called *Universität, Technische Universität* or *Technische Hochschule*) and polytechnics (*Fachhochschulen*). The latter offer shorter and more vocationally orientated courses, and can be entered directly with a leaving qualification from some forms of vocational training (notably the *Fachoberschulreife*), as well as with the *Abitur*. There are around 1·2 million students in universities and 350,000 students at the polytechnics. Student numbers (in West Germany) have risen by 50 per cent since 1980, and have more than doubled since the early 1970s, giving rise to enormous pressures within the system and its financing (see 'Reform proposals' below).

There is continuing discussion about widening the entrance requirements for entry into university to encompass a broader range of vocational training qualifications. At present, individuals with a vocational training qualification can attend a range of courses, including evening classes at a *Gymnasium*, to acquire the equivalent of the *Abitur* and gain entrance to university (the so-called 'second route' to higher education). The individual *Länder* determine the way this actually works, and can set entrance exams or other selection criteria for university entrance.

Students attend university for much longer than in the UK, with an average five or six years to first degree at a university, though four years is more usual at a polytechnic.

Students are generally financed by their parents or work during their studies (and in vacations). There is a system of loans for those from lower-income families, and around 400,000 students are in receipt of loans.

Universities. In theory, possession of the *Abitur* confers the right not only to higher education but also to a free choice of subject, irrespective of earlier specialization. In practice the large numbers of young people passing the *Abitur* compared with the limited number of places available in some popular specialisms have led universities to introduce a form of selection, the *numerus clausus*, by which certain grades are required at *Abitur* level. Whether courses need to be regulated by selection, and how selection is to be organized, are decided by a central inter-*Land* body, the ZVS (Zentralstelle für Vergabe von Studientplätzen). The *numerus clausus* applies particularly in vocationally orientated university courses (architecture, medicine, veterinary science, dentistry and, since 1990, in management science – *Betriebswirtschaftlehre*). Drop-out rates tend to be higher in the arts subjects, where there is no *numerus clausus*. For example, the drop-out rate after two years in the arts is around 30 per cent. Overall, according to OECD figures, 87 per cent of students are still in full-time higher education three years after matriculation.

Besides the state-run universities there are a large number of private higher education institutions, some of which provide technical or business education. (A guide is available from the Federal Ministry of Education and Science.) They include a branch of the European Business School at Oestrich-Winkel, the Koblenz School of Management, a banking college (Hochschule für Bankwirtschaft) in Frankfurt, the Private University of Witten/Herdecke, and numerous specialist institutions in technical areas and design.

There is no established hierarchy of universities. Meagre state support for students means that many continue to live at home, or near by, and the relative dispersal of the population into a number of conurbations has encouraged strong, well respected universities throughout the country. However, individual departments or professors may acquire a strong reputation and these may be sought out by prospective students and employers alike.

Polytechnics. The polytechnics (*Fachhochschulen*) were established in the 1960s. Their graduates generally attract slightly lower starting salaries than university graduates. But the more practical nature of their education, the effective use of work placements, and the fact that many polytechnic students have already completed initial vocational training and shown their determination to pursue higher education make them attractive to many employers, especially in small and medium-sized companies. On completion of their course (see below), polytechnic students can go on to university with credits for courses.

Higher education qualifications. Degree subjects are divided into two phases: a foundation period (*Grundstudium*) of four to five semesters, leading to an intermediate qualification, the *Vordiplom*. This is followed by the main degree course, usually lasting a minimum of four semesters, but typically longer. The first degree-level qualification awarded in universities in most specialisms is the *Diplom* (written Dipl. Ing., Dipl. Kaufmann, etc.) In certain areas of study where the main employer is the state, such as teaching, students take a qualification termed the *Staatsexamen* instead. In some arts subjects, universities may offer an MA as an alternative to the *Staatsexamen* for students who do not wish to enter the public service.

The polytechnics award a *Diplom* for all courses, usually written as Dipl. (FH) to distinguish it from a university diploma.

Universities and polytechnics both offer courses in management science, with the qualification either of *Diplom-Kaufmann* or *Diplom-Betriebswirtschaft*. Business studies combined with engineering, leading to the qualification of *Wirtschaftsingenieur* are another common starting point for a career in management. (See also 'Management training' below).

The *Diplom* usually entails the preparation of a dissertation, some written examinations and an oral. The choice of dissertation subject (with research in some fields carried out during a company placement – with subsequent useful contacts) may be important in later recruitment to management positions.

Postgraduate work leading to a doctorate is confined to universities, and German output of doctoral graduates is considerably higher than in the UK. Doctoral qualifications figure prominently among senior public figures and managers of very large enterprises, especially in technical areas, and PhDs in some fields can command a very high salary premium on initial recruitment.

MBAs are taught only at the Schiller International University, Heidelberg, and at the Armed Services University in Munich, in association with Henley Management College. There is concern among practitioners about the quality of some European MBAs, and only the top 20 or so business schools are well-regarded.

Criticisms and proposals for reform. German universities have been described as 'the weak link in German education . . . mostly overcrowded, inefficient and dispiriting for students' (*Financial Times*, 6 September 1991). The basic difficulty stems from a combination of factors: a tradition of liberal education, with extensive freedom for students to choose and switch subjects, long study periods of up to seven years to first-degree level (often necessitated by the need to finance study through periodic paid work), a demographically based surge of students in the 1980s, and increasing numbers of school students passing the *Abitur* and acquiring the right to enrol at a university.

Proposals for reform have come from various quarters. Most have proved highly controversial. They include:

- Opportunities for shortening or speeding up the period of study, in particular for more vocationally orientated courses, including slimming down the curricula in some areas.
- Greater opportunities for subsequent development as a corollary of shorter study periods.
- Rationalization of the administrative and political framework, and generally tighter management of physical and human resources (i.e. professors).
- More rigorous selection at university entrance to cut overall numbers and reduce the drop-out rate.

Initial vocational training

The core of Germany's system of initial vocational training is the statutory 'dual system' in which on-the-job training under the supervision of qualified employees is combined with off-the-job training in special vocational schools (*Berufsschulen*), of which there are approximately 1,500 in the former Federal Republic. Young people may enter the system from any of the three basic types of school described above. For example, around a quarter of young people holding an *Abitur* qualification, giving access to higher education, initially enter the vocational training system, mostly in white-collar occupations, and subsequently look for a university place.

In all just over 70 per cent of young people enter the dual system, excluding apprenticeship drop-outs. Drop-out rates are low, and various schemes exist to catch those falling through the net up to the age of 19.

Attendance at a *Berufsschule*, providing general as well as narrowly vocational education, is obligatory for all young people aged between 16 and 18 not otherwise in full-time education.

The provision of training places is entirely the responsibility of employers: there is no obligation to train and no formal right to vocational training. Whereas the number of training places on offer in the early 1980s frequently fell short of the number of young people looking for vocational training, by the early 1990s there was an excess of places on offer. In 1991, for example, employers in what used to be the Federal Republic notified some 711,000 new training places to the Federal Employment Institute (the job placement and training authority – see below) for which there were ultimately 540,000 new training contracts started. According to the Education Ministry's 1992 annual report, this reflected demographic changes and increasing numbers of school leavers moving into technical training or higher education. Substantial numbers of young people from the former German Democratic Republic (East Germany) also took up training places in the west, especially in areas close to the old border. In all, in 1990, some 1,480,000 young people were in the dual system, 42 per cent of them women.

However, there is a serious shortage of training places in the old East Germany, only partly alleviated by opportunities in those West German regions bordering the east. Some 120,000–130,000 young people were expected to be looking for a training place in 1992/93 in the east, with only about 60,000 workplace trainee vacancies on offer by firms. The new east German *Land* governments have developed a range of programmes to complement federal efforts and provide subsidies for training in workplaces; they include one-off grants of DM 5,000 (£2,000) together with on-going finance to cover up to 75 per cent of trainees' pay.

Why train? Accreditation as a training firm offers a number of advantages to an employer. In a society where job mobility has traditionally been lower than in the UK, access to a home-grown pool of skilled workers, not only trained in specific skills but also socialized into the company's culture, is a competitive advantage, especially if the labour market is tight. Many larger companies often train considerably more workers than they immediately need, guaranteeing themselves a choice of the best of the bunch and releasing trained employees into the rest of the economy without the implication of poaching or wage competition. Firms may not employ *young people* in any of the accredited occupations unless they offer training on the terms specified by the Vocational Training Act. Employers who need and want to recruit good-quality young people must offer training opportunities, and a well developed training programme is seen as part of developing a positive corporate image.

As well as providing a supply of skilled workers across a broad range of occupations, with benefits for product quality and service explored in the UK by numerous publications from the National Institute of Economic and Social Research, the generally high standard of training also imparts foundation skills which favour the later training of foremen and supervisors (*Meister* – see below).

Training establishments

Companies must meet certain minimum criteria to win approval as a training company (set out in articles 20–4 and 70–96 of the Federal Vocational Training Act). Apart from providing the appropriate facilities, a company wishing to take on trainees must demonstrate that it employs suitably qualified instructors who meet the requirements laid down by the Economics Ministry for the occupations offered for training. The instructors typically include people over the age of 24 who have passed a master craftsmen's examination (*Meisterprüfung*), completed vocational training in a relevant occupation and have shown evidence of suitability, with a higher education qualification or professional qualification in a relevant occupation and evidence of practical experience. Instructors must pass an aptitude test, which is part of the *Meister* examination in most craft trades.

The Vocational Training Act also regulates training requirements in such professions as the law, accountancy and medicine.

Training takes place in some 380 classified occupations. Although many English-language publications refer to 'apprenticeships', the German term for apprentice (*Lehrling*) was in fact replaced by the term 'trainee' (*Auszubildende*; *Azubi* for short) some years ago. Around 125 of the classified occupations are in craft trades.

Competent bodies

Each of the components of the dual system is the responsibility of a different political authority. On-the-job training is regulated by the Federal Vocational Training Act (*Berufsbildungsgesetz*), 1969, and is the responsibility of central government, acting on the advice of the tripartite Federal Institute of Vocational Training. Off-the-job training in the vocational schools comes under the authority of the *Länder*. Co-ordination between the *Länder* is achieved through a standing conference of their Ministers of Education.

At regional level within each *Land* a major role in the supervision and organization of training is played by the chambers of industry and commerce (*Industrie-und Handelskammern*), which are assigned the role of 'competent body' at local level under the Vocational Training Act. The chambers embrace not only industry and commerce, but also the liberal professions, crafts (*Handwerke*) and agriculture. Membership of an appropriate chamber is compulsory for any undertaking trading in Germany, and companies engaged in specific recognized occupations must employ appropriately qualified staff (in the crafts usually bearing the title *Meister*).

The role of the chambers is to enforce registration requirements, oversee training at company level, register training agreements, advise on the operation of the system, organize examinations and validate the vocational training qualifications.

The training relationship

The basis of the training relationship is the training agreement between the employer and the trainee. Under the requirements of the Vocational Training Act, the training contract must be in writing and must specify the main terms and conditions of employment during the period of training: the Act lists such elements as the division of the working week between on-the-job activity and attendance at a vocational training school, and other off-the-job training measures, the length of the probationary period, pay, holiday entitlement and terms for terminating the trainee contract.

Trainees' pay is customarily set by collective agreement, although companies may pay more if they wish. Pay rises during the three or four-year period of training but is still substantially below full-time adult rates. In the first half of 1992 first-year monthly trainee rates in manufacturing industry in West Germany ranged between DM 800 and DM 900 (£320–£360), rising to DM 1,000–DM 1,150 (£400–£460) in the fourth year of training. In the east, rates varied between DM 445 (£178) and DM 600 (£240) in the first year of training.

The training agreement also sets out the mutual obligations of the employer and trainee once training has begun. Specifically, the employer (or an assigned training provider) is required to ensure that the specified skills and knowledge are imparted to the trainee to ensure that the object of training (the qualification) is achieved, and to provide all the tools, equipment and other training resources free of charge to the trainee, both for on-the-job training and for the purpose of examinations. The employer must guarantee appropriate time off for attending a vocational school, and ensure that the trainee attends. Trainees may be assigned only to tasks which serve the aims of the training and are within the trainee's physical capacity. At the end of the period of training the employer must issue a certificate specifying the type, length and purpose of the training, the skills and knowledge acquired, and, if the trainee requests it, a report on conduct, performance and specialist abilities.

Vocational training schools and training centres

The *Berufsschulen*, administered by the respective *Land* governments, provide the theoretical element of vocational training within the dual system, as well as offering a basic vocational training preparatory course for those leaving school but lacking basic attainments. In addition, trainees in the dual system continue to receive an element of general education, which accounts for about 40 per cent of the time spent in the vocational schools. Instruction in vocational schools is typically on a daily basis (with one or two days' tuition per week) combined with full-time block release.

The craft training schools, *Berufsfachschulen*, can supplement or replace company training for people in the dual system, and train young people for the qualifications awarded by the chambers of commerce. Around 12 per cent of those in the 16–19 age group are in full-time vocational training in one of the *Berufsfachschulen*, particularly in specialisms where on-the-job training might be inappropriate. In contrast to entry into the dual system and the *Berufsschulen*, entry to a *Berufsfachschule* requires a secondary school leaving certificate.

Where companies are small, or cannot offer a full range of experience to meet training requirements (on practical or safety grounds, or in sectors where technical change is especially fast), resort is often had to inter-company training centres (*überbetriebliche Ausbildungsstätten*), which complement the theoretical activity of the vocational school with a broader range of directed on-the-job experience. The centres are usually financed by employer associations, with supplementary funding from public authorities, and may serve a broad spectrum of training objectives (such as for managers) as well as initial vocational training.

Length of training

Training lasts between two and three and a half years, depending on industry and occupation.

Cost of training

The costs of training in-plant are borne solely by companies themselves. They may also bear a proportion of the cost of any inter-company training facilities. Vocational schools are paid for by the *Länder*.
It is estimated that total company spending within the dual system
stood at DM 23,000 million (£9·2 billion) in 1990.

Some state aid is available to finance the training of young people
who need preparatory training on leaving school before entering the
dual system, or to meet other special needs (see below, on the services
of the Bundesanstalt für Arbeit).

Type of qualification

Basic vocational training takes place in one of the 380 or so occupations recognized by the authorities. Over the past twenty years the
number of recognized occupations has fallen from around 600 in 1971,
as training is nowadays more comprehensive within broader occupational categories. Training must confer transferable skills, and may not
be related solely to a company's particular skill requirements.

There is considerable debate about the promotion of 'strategic skills'
at the level of both initial and continuing vocational training.

Occupations become recognized as such by the Economics Ministry
in collaboration with the Ministry of Education and Science. The training regulations for each occupation specify the name of the occupation,
the length of training, the nature of the skills and knowledge required,
instructions on training content and the overall training plan for the
course, and the examination requirements. The detailed organization of
examinations, and validation of qualifications, are the responsibility of
the chambers of commerce (see above). Examination is by boards of
part-time examiners. Trainees are examined in a written test, an oral
test and a practical test. Trainees may not proceed to take the test
unless they have kept proper records of their activities during the
period of training.

There is a degree of flexibility in the system, and the content and
form of training may be revised in consultation with employers' organizations, trade unions and the training and education authorities, with
the impetus usually coming from the two sides of industry. For example,
the training syllabus for the metalworking industry (including electrical
engineering and electronics) was comprehensively overhauled in the

late 1980s and the commercial syllabus is currently undergoing a major reform.

On passing the final examination, trainees receive certificates setting out the grades, the official title of the qualification and the company where the training took place.

By sector, in 1990, 51 per cent of training places were in industry and commerce, 33 per cent in the traditional craft sector (*Handwerk*) most nearly corresponding to the traditional notion of apprenticeship, 9 per cent in the self-employed occupations, and the balance in the public sector, agriculture, domestic service and the merchant navy.

The most popular areas were: for men – vehicle mechanic, electrical installation, sales specialist (*Kaufmann*) wholesale/foreign trade, industrial mechanic, joiner, basic banking qualification (*Bankkaufmann*) and business specialist, industrial production and sales (*Industriekaufmann*). For women they were: hairdressing (7 per cent of all trainees), the retail trade, commercial clerk (*Bürokauffrau*), general practitioner's assistant, business specialist, industry, dentist's assistant, and sales specialist for food products.

After initial training

On completion of initial training, just under 50 per cent of trainees take a permanent job in the occupation for which they were trained, around 85 per cent with the company that trained them. Ten per cent then do their military service (or alternative civic service). Some 10 per cent become unemployed, and 13 per cent go on to further training or education. The remainder either work in some new field or take up a fixed-term contract, increasingly common in German since 1985 legislation eased the requirements (see *Recruitment* in this series).

Criticisms

The dual system has been criticized for some of its rigidities:

- The lengthy period needed to acquire basic skills.
- Too much theoretical training, with the looming prospect of serious shortages of instructors.
- General inflexibility.
- Lack of co-ordination between examining bodies leading to inconsistent standards.

Many of these points are outweighed by the sheer comprehensiveness of the system, the fact that the academically less gifted acquire some status and prestige through recognized training, and the creation of a deep pool of skills and work attitudes which allow the delivery of more complex and efficient goods and services at all levels. (See, for example, the comparative sectoral NIESR studies on furniture making and the hotel industry.) Steps have been taken towards greater flexibility, for example by reducing the number of training occupations in each sector and broadening the range of skills.

In industry the high level of training of skilled workers, combined with a large pool of qualified foremen (see below), has been identified as enabling highly qualified technicians or graduate engineers to avoid the need to become involved in day-to-day troubleshooting on the shop floor, as compared with experience reported in the UK.

Technical and further training

Technical and further vocational training is also available for people with a basic vocational qualification in a variety of vocational training schools. These include trade schools (*Fachschulen*), vocational further education colleges (*Berufsaufbauschulen*) and vocational colleges (*Fachoberschulen*). Whilst some of these institutions offer training for the job of foreman or technician, others provide enhanced basic vocational skills and issue their own qualifications, which can be used to gain entry to a polytechnic (*Fachhochschule* – see above), ultimately offering an alternative route into tertiary education.

Training of technicians and supervisors (Meister). Individuals with an initial vocational qualification and an appropriate period of experience prescribed by the Vocational Training Act, usually three years, can proceed to acquire more advanced qualifications across the range of industrial, craft and commercial occupations. The best-known title, *Meister*, is found both in craft occupations (*Handwerk*) and in industry (with the qualification *Industrie-Meister*). Those undertaking further training in commerce, which includes areas such as data processing, will earn a title such as *Fachkaufmann, Fachwirt* or *Betriebswirt*.

Training at a *Berufsfachschule* for the status of technician holding a formal technical qualification (*staatlich geprüfter Techniker*) is open to individuals who have completed initial vocational training and gained two years' experience.

Training, which may be full or part-time, is undertaken at a special trade school (*Fachschule*), with trainees meeting their own costs, though with some state help available from the federal employment service (see below). The period of training is one to two years full-time or three years part-time.

In 1990 around 51,000 people entered for *Meister* examinations in the craft trades, of whom 75 per cent passed. A further 50,000 undertook further training in commercial occupations (66 per cent pass rate) and 17,000 in industrial and technical professions (85 per cent pass rate).

A number of UK-based studies have identified the high level of training of German first-line managers, and the availability of a large number of such individuals in industry, as a vital component in manufacturing success (see 'Further reading').

Training and the official employment service

As well as running the official job placement service and providing careers advice and job counselling, the federal employment service also offers a number of training opportunities to employers and employees. (The service is administered by the Federal Labour Institute, the Bundesanstalt für Arbeit or BfA, based in Nuremberg). As well as its more conventional training activities in West Germany, the BfA is also centrally involved in running job creation schemes and training in East Germany.

The promotion of vocational training is a statutory obligation on the BfA under the Work Promotion Act (*Arbeitsförderungsgesetz*), 1969. It may carry out training itself, make use of the training facilities of other public institutions, or resort to other training providers. The main areas covered are as follows.

Vocational training for individuals

Grants or advances are available to enable individuals to participate in vocational training, if either the individual situation of the prospective trainee or the location of the training creates financial or practical difficulties. Grants may cover items such as tools, equipment and clothing, travel expenses if the training is not near by, and a maintenance allowance for trainees who do not live with their parents. (The grants are means-tested, except for individuals who have been in paid employment for at least one year or who are unemployed.)

' As well as initial or further vocational training, BfA grants can also be used to enable individuals to obtain a secondary school leaving certificate (*Hauptschulabschluß*), which is a prerequisite for entering the 'dual system', or to remedy any other general educational short-comings which handicap the individual's chances on the labour market.

Further vocational training

The BfA can support further vocational training for individuals who have completed a course of initial vocational training followed by three years' work, or six years' work experience. The criteria for support are whether the course:

- Offers scope for individual advancement.
- Adapts existing skills to labour-market or job requirements.
- Enables an unemployed or older person to get a job.
- Assists in the development of training instructors.

Support takes the form of grants to meet costs, together with a subsistence allowance for full-time trainees amounting to 65 per cent of former income (less statutory deductions), raised to 73 per cent when there are dependants. Loans are also available.

Retraining

Grants and subsistence allowances are also available to support individuals to undergo retraining or to enable an employee to move to alternative employment and further occupational mobility and flexibility.

Grants are available to employers to enable them to finance a period of introductory training for the unemployed, or those threatened with unemployment. Subsidies paid by the BfA to the employer can cover up to 50 per cent of the usual agreed or local rate for the job, and may be paid for up to one year.

Promotion of vocational training institutions

The BfA can provide grants and loans for the construction, expansion and equipping of vocational training institutions. These include the inter-company training centres referred to in connection with the 'dual system' above, as well as other facilities provided by bodies such as chambers of trade and commerce, employer associations and employees' organizations and welfare societies. Organizations entitled to seek financial support may not, however, be engaged in training on a commercial basis, nor must they be predominantly intended to serve the training needs of a single establishment or organization.

Managerial training and development

Management training

Compared with the UK, top managers in German business, particularly in large companies, are more likely to be graduates of universities or polytechnics. Given the length of their education, together with military service in the case of men, graduates recruited into business are likely to be at least 26 and probably nearer 28 (30 if they have a doctorate). Board members of large companies, especially in fields such as chemicals, are frequently educated to doctoral level, and a doctorate in engineering is a common route to senior management throughout manufacturing industry. Nearly two-thirds of top managers are educated to degree level (including polytechnic graduates), compared with about half in the UK.

Whereas larger companies are more inclined to recruit from universities, amongst which there is no established hierarchy, small and medium-sized companies often opt for graduates from the polytechnics (*Fachhochschulen*). In the first place, they may well have entered higher education through the route of a completed apprenticeship rather than the *Abitur*, and secondly their studies will have been more directly vocationally relevant (see above, 'Tertiary education').

The subjects studied have much greater relevance to recruitment than in the UK, and liberal arts graduates tend to move into teaching rather than enter management. In the past, few German managers changed company to obtain promotion, and the vast bulk of senior appointments were filled internally. Managers were therefore recruited after a solid academic performance or from among capable skilled workers with *Meister* qualification, and developed internally. Since there were also well established business and management studies options at universities and polytechnics, there was little demand for a transferable managerial qualification such as the MBA. The weakening of this culture somewhat during the 1980s may well have raised the attraction of an MBA qualification at an American or leading European business school. MBAs are seen as an attractive qualification for individuals looking to a career in consultancy or a strategic role in a large company.

Post-entry practice varies considerably, depending on the size of the company and the management area into which the graduate is recruited. Specific trainee programmes tend to be reserved for graduates entering general management and identified as strong performers, and to be confined to large companies. However, the competition for good-quality graduates in the late 1980s and early 1990s – principally due to demographic shifts combined with a phase of strong economic growth – has led firms to improve their public presentation and highlight their development opportunities for graduates.

Management development

Managerial development, especially for those just above first-line supervisor level, is widespread, in particular for developing technical knowledge and skills as well as managerial capacity.

In the absence of business schools and university departments offering development courses, firms are obliged either to provide their own programmes or to turn to the multitude of external training providers. The business daily *Handelsblatt* produces an annual survey of management training courses (generically termed *Weiterbildung*). Chambers of commerce also offer management development courses and seminars.

Compared with other employees, managers enjoy a much greater intensity of post-entry training and development. A survey by the journal *Management Wissen* (now a supplement in the weekly *Wirtschaftswoche*) showed that companies identified the greatest areas of training need for managers as: controlling, marketing, the management of innovation, social/personal development and employee development.

Continuing training

Continuing training covers an enormously wide spectrum of activities, including those already referred to above as promoted by the BfA and the training of *Meister*, and takes place in a multitude of institutions as well as via distance learning. Aspects of continuing training which have become a focus of collective bargaining are discussed below (see 'Agreed training provision'). Continuing training in Germany has been referred to as 'untransparent' because of the diversity of institutional arrangements, aims and implementing regulations. Chambers of trade and commerce (in particular their central organizations; see appendix 4.2) and the BfA hold databases of training opportunities, and can provide advice. The BfA has two databases, for example: Kurs and an on-line system Kurs-Direkt.

In order to set standards for private training providers, the BfA has also developed a set of criteria for quality assurance known as FuU standards.

Continuing training may be carried out in-house, through a public training facility, or through a commercial organization that provides training.

In 1988 (the most recent year for which survey data are available), 18 per cent of West Germans participated in some form of continuing vocational training. In general the rate of participation increased with educational level: 40 per cent of those with tertiary education, for example, undertook some continuing training, compared with 20 per cent holding only an initial training qualification.

Workforce consultation

Under the Works Constitution Act, 1972, works councils and the employer are required to co-operate in the field of, and promote, vocational training; works councils have a right of codetermination in some areas. (On the broader rights of works councils, see *Industrial Relations* in this series.) This encompasses a number of training issues:

- Both parties are required to ensure full access to training opportunities, within and outside the firm, and in particular to attend to the training needs of older employees.
- Employers must consult works councils on training facilities and schemes.
- Works councils have a right of codetermination in the implementation of workplace training. If there is disagreement a conciliation

committee set up under works council legislation can issue a binding ruling.

- Works councils may demand the recall or non-appointment of any person charged with training duties who they feel is not suitably qualified (in the terms of the Vocational Training Act). In the event of disagreement the works council can apply to the labour courts for a ruling.
- Works councils have a right to put forward proposals as to which individuals or groups of employees should participate in training opportunities. Again, a conciliation committee can decide in the event of failure to agree.

Under dismissal protection legislation, employers are also required to consider whether an employee about to be dismissed could work elsewhere in the establishment after a reasonable period of training or retraining.

Agreed training provision

As noted above, the issue of continuing training has grown in importance in recent years, becoming a focus of trade union as well as employer and government activity and consideration. Continuing training, for example, is at the heart of the reforms outlined by the metalworkers' union IG Metall in its proposal *Tarifreform 2000*. This document seeks to address a number of issues in the development of collective bargaining over the coming decade, and assigns considerable importance to moves towards skill-based pay structures and continuing training and development.

Although there are trade union hopes of a greater training content for collective bargaining in the future, to complement existing union influence in the organization of initial training under the 'dual system', as yet detailed sectoral provisions are rare and raise problems of implementation at workplace level. Moreover, although employers appear willing to commit substantial funds to in-company training of their specialists and managers, there is less enthusiasm for broadening less skilled workers' training, as called for by the trade unions.

A recent trade union study identified a number of current provisions and approaches (see R. Bispinck, 'Qualifikation und Qualifizierung in Tarifverträgen', *WSI-Mitteilungen* 6, 1992):

Minimum training levels for grading purposes. These figure in most industry agreements, and specify the possession of formal qualifications as a prerequisite of admission to certain pay grades.

Training and technical change. Some agreements require an employer engaged in rationalization and job cuts to examine the possibility of continued employment for employees upon retraining. These agreements are often accompanied by maintenance of earnings agreements of either limited or, in some sectors, unlimited duration. As noted above, German law on redundancies can impose this requirement on an employer: since any redundancy must be 'socially warranted', an employer may not have a free hand in selecting employees for redundancy, and such clauses therefore may take on particular relevance.

Skill development. The above defensive approach is also complemented, in some agreements, by a more forward-looking concern to develop employee skills. One pioneer agreement in this respect was the Wage and Salary Framework Agreement (*Lohn- und Gehaltsrahmentarifvertrag I*) covering the 145,000 employees in the metalworking industry in North Württemberg and North Baden, agreed in 1988. As well as setting out the overall framework of grading and job evaluation, the agreement emphasizes the need to develop and extend occupational skills. Section 3 of the agreement requires the employer to assess the need for training and discuss training needs with works councils. An assessment of the firm's training requirements must be undertaken annually; in addition, consideration must be given to the broader training needs of the work force. Employees who receive training are entitled to be regraded if appropriate, provided the newly acquired skill is put into practice. Measures aimed at general further training, which are not directly related to the employer's training needs, and management seminars are excluded. Despite the forward-looking nature of the agreement, it has not as yet been extended to the metalworking industry in other regions and the take-up of its provisions at company level is reported to be fairly low.

An agreement concluded at Shell AG in 1988 provides for a range of training opportunities aimed at 'broadening the occupational and personal capabilities of the employee', with training carried out not during agreed working time but by using time 'released' though cuts in working hours.

Time-off rights for education

Paid educational leave has been legislated for in the majority of *Länder* in West Germany. For example, the 1985 Employees' Continuing Education Act (*Arbeitnehmerweiterbildungsgesetz*) in North Rhine–Westphalia provides for five days' leave a year to allow participation in 'vocational and civic education' on full pay at recognized educational and training institutions.

The interpretation of such legislation has caused problems, because of disputes over which courses are admissible. In North Rhine–Westphalia agreement was reached in 1990 between the *Land* organizations of trade unions and employers which provided that:

- Courses had to be recognized by the *Land* authorities and must take place in recognized institutions.
- Vocational training need not be confined to the employees' immediate workplace, and may include the acquisition of key skills such as computing or foreign languages.
- Civic education embraces 'the acquisition and extension of knowledge of political and social structures and the capacity to participate in social and political life'. However, courses solely targeted at trade union education and training for the exercise of union functions are not included.
- Courses must in principle be open to all comers, and information on them must be accessible.

In addition to these statutory rights for all employees, elected members of works councils who are released from work to attend courses relevant to their duties are entitled to paid time off. Education for works councillors can be provided by trade unions, but employers may also offer training in such issues as job evaluation (as grading is subject to consultation). Moreover, all works council members – whether full-time or not – are entitled to three weeks' paid time off during their four-year period of office.

Financing

The costs of initial training and continuing training are borne wholly by the employer. Total spending under the dual system by companies was estimated at DM 23 billion (£9.2 billion) in 1990. There are no levies or mandatory requirements on levels of training expenditure. However, there are mandatory requirements on employing only time-served apprentices and *Meister* in certain trades. The Bundesanstalt für Arbeit provides funds for the training or retraining of both the employed and the unemployed, and provides grants and subsidies to employers and other organizations to help them extend training facilities and opportunities (see above).

Although the public authorities and federal employment service jointly devote large sums to financing continuing training, as with initial training the vast bulk of finance comes from industry. In 1988, for example, industry spent some DM 39 billion (£15·6 billion) on continuing training, compared with public spending of DM 9 billion (£5·4 billion). German unification has massively raised public spending on training and employment measures in the new *Länder*, although cuts in the BfA's budget could threaten some programmes.

Appendix 4.1 Educational attainment

Level	Percentage of 25–64 age group
Lower secondary	22
Upper secondary	61
Higher education (non-university)	7
University	10

Source: OECD.

Appendix 4.2 Organizations

Federal Ministry of Labour
(Bundesministerium für Arbeit und Sozialordnung):
5300 Bonn 1
Rochustraße 1
tel. + 49 228 5271

Federal Ministry of Education and Science (Bundesministerium für Bildung und Wissenschaft):
Postfach 20 01 08
5300 Bonn 2
tel. + 49 228 571

Federal Employment Institute
(Bundesanstalt für Arbeit, BfA):
Regensburgerstraße 104
8500 Nürnberg 30
tel. + 49 911 170
fax + 49 911 17 21 23

Federal Institute of Vocational
Training (Bundesinstitut für
Berufsbildung):
Fehrbelliner Platz 3
1000 Berlin 31
tel. + 49 30 868 31

German Society of Personnel
Management (Deutsche Gesellschaft
für Personalführung, DGFP):
4000 Düsseldorf 1
Niederkasseler Lohweg 16
tel. + 49 211 59 78 0
fax + 49 211 59 78 505

German Chamber of Industry and
Commerce (Deutscher Industrie und
Handelstag):
Postfach 1446
Adenauerallee 148
5300 Bonn 1
tel. + 49 228 1040

British–German School of
Vocational Training:
17–18 Haywards Place
Clerkenwell Green
London EC1R 0EQ

Established via an initiative of the
German Chamber of Commerce in
London, the school offers dual
German-UK qualifications
(*Kaufmann* and BTEC HND) in a
range of subjects for employees of
member companies of the organiza-
tion.

Handelsblatt *Jahrbuch Weiterbildung*
(annual survey of management
training):
Kasernenstraße 67
Postfach 10 11 02
4000 Düsseldorf 1
tel. + 49 211 8 87 0
fax + 49 211 32 67 59

Chapter 5

Greece

Initial vocational training takes place primarily in public institutions, either in the form of technical and vocational education within schools or through apprenticeships organized via the state employment service, OAED. Although on-the-job and continuing training has been at a low level in the bulk of the small and medium-sized enterprises which make up the Greek economy, European Community funds have stimulated greater interest among larger and more export-orientated firms. The trade unions have also identified training as a national priority, and training issues have recently begun to figure on the bargaining agenda for the first time.

The educational system

The nine-year compulsory education consists of six years of primary (*Demotico*) and three years of lower-cycle secondary (*Gymnasio*) education. On completion of compulsory education, school-leavers are awarded a diploma (*Apolyterio*).

Upper secondary education

Apart from joining the labour market, they then choose either to continue their general education or to engage in vocational education/training. Four options are available:

- General Secondary Education (*Lykeio*).
- Technical-Vocational *Lykeio* (TEL).
- Integrated Comprehensive *Lykeio* (EPL).
- Technical-Vocational School (TES) and an apprenticeship under the auspices of the official employment and training agency, OAED.

The three-year *General Lykeio* provides a general education for those *Gymnasio* graduates – up to 18 years old – who wish to continue their studies at the tertiary level. Young people who are older or who work during the day can attend evening General *Lykeio*, where the period of study, with a shorter teaching timetable, is four years. This level includes an initial common curriculum followed by a core curriculum, with four special options in maths and physics, the physical and biological sciences, classics and literature, and mathematics/history/sociology, which leads to economics and business studies. At the end of the third year all students sit the examinations for the school leaving certificate (*Apolyterio* – comparable to GCSE standard, grades A, B, C). A pass in the *Apolyterio* allows students of the four streams to sit the general entrance examinations, held in late June, for a place in higher education.

Candidates can apply to up to sixty different departments of various institutions (including the military academies of all branches). Each year a quota is announced for every department in higher education. Selection is based on performance in the general entrance examinations as well as on the order of preference of each department that the student wishes to attend.

Candidates who fail to gain entry to higher education can resit at least one subject the following year. After two unsuccessful attempts they have to resit all subjects. Alternatively, they can enter the labour market, or join the second year of a Technical–Vocational *Lykeio* or the first year of a Technical–Vocational School, or study at an institution of tertiary education outside the general examination system.

The Technical–Vocational Lykeio (TEL) provides general and vocational education. The duration of studies is three years for *Gymnasio* graduates and two years for graduates of any other type of *Lykeio*. Evening courses are also available for four or three years respectively. In the first year, students are taught general subjects for twenty-one teaching hours a week and special subjects, common to all, for thirteen hours. In the second year they attend common general subjects for nineteen hours per week and fifteen hours of vocational specialisms, which they chose from a range of options.

In the third year TEL students attend general subjects for thirteen hours a week and can either specialize further in an area of their vocational sector (e.g. agriculture and cattle breeding or floriculture) for twenty-one hours a week, or choose one of the three streams available to them (A, B or D) in order to sit the general examinations.

TEL graduates receive either a specialization 'degree' (*Ptychio*) or a diploma (*Apolyterio*) for those who chose a stream. *Ptychio* holders have the following options:

- Join the labour market, equipped with the vocational training they received at school.
- Continue in higher education at the Technical Education Institutions (TEI), without examinations, for a percentage of the seats available. Selection is based on the total points each graduate has gathered.
- Change specialization area, within the same sector, by enrolling in the third year or change sector by attending the second and third years again.

Apolyterio holders can:

- Sit the general examinations.
- Continue at the Technical Education Institutions (TEI), without examinations, on the basis of their scholastic performance, as described above for the *Ptychio* holders.
- Enrol again at the third year to obtain a specialization degree in the sector they chose in their second year.

Technical–Vocational Schools (TES) train their students in specific occupations. They are integrated with the TELs (as described above), forming Vocational and Technical Training Centres (KETEK). Courses last two years (three at the evening schools). In the first year, students choose to specialize in one of fourteen vocational options (depending on the availability of the sector in a TES). The options include industrial skills (together with electronics), craft skills (gold and silversmithing, watchmaking), commerce and agriculture.

In the second year TES students pursue their area of specialization further. Out of a total of thirty teaching hours per week, six are devoted to general educational subjects and twenty-four to vocational specialisms. Complementary in-company training is also available to TES students, on a non-compulsory basis, for a limited period of three months. However, since it is practically impossible for such a large number of work placements to be secured, few students are able to take advantage of such a scheme.

TES graduates can join the labour market or the second year of a TEL if they want to continue their studies at tertiary level.

The Integrated Comprehensive Lykeio (EPL), also called 'Unified Multidisciplinary *Lykeio*', is the most recently established form of *Lykeio*. In 1984 the first fourteen EPLs were opened, with 4,458 students. In 1986 enrolment reached 15,565 students in twenty-two EPLs.

EPLs provide both general education and vocational training. There is a core curriculum, together with options in health, the natural sciences and social welfare, economics and management, together with technical subjects. EPL graduates can attend any institution of tertiary education outside the general examination system. Alternatively, they may move straight to the labour market or acquire additional vocational training.

The *OAED apprenticeship* is provided by the Organization for Manpower and Employment (OAED). It is the only programme that combines vocational education with practical on-the-job training.

In 1990 around 11,000 students were attending courses in forty-five Technical-Vocational Training Centres (KETEK) throughout Greece, and in 1991 4,753 new students were admitted. When applications exceed the number of places available (as is usually the case in most centres), candidates are selected by interview. The apprenticeship lasts up to three years (six terms) and is based on the 'dual system'. In the first year students attend lectures and workshops in the Apprenticeship Centres on a full-time basis (thirty-seven hours a week, five days a week). In the second and third years students attend lectures in the centres and also undergo practical in-company training, which grows in importance throughout the course, reaching 100 per cent of attendance time in the final term. Each year the OAED places 8,000 apprentices in companies.

Apprentices are paid by their employer, in accordance with youth pay rates (50 per cent of the national minimum wage in the first term, on a sliding scale up to 100 per cent in the sixth) as laid down by the national collective agreement. They also have full medical and hospital insurance, the cost of which is at first covered wholly by the OAED (in the first year) and subsequently by the employer. Moreover, for those away from home, the OAED provides free board and lodging or free meal vouchers where no facilities are available (1,000 and 3,000 students, respectively, were covered by these schemes in 1990).

Apprenticeship graduates join the labour market. The apprenticeship is not directly linked with the rest of the secondary education, and qualified apprentices cannot join the educational system at a level higher than they left it at.

Other institutions of secondary education. Alongside the above institutions, a number of others, of lesser importance – at least in quantitative terms – operate:

- The *Classical Lykeio*, with an emphasis on the classics and humanities.
- The *Greek Merchant Navy Lykeio for Officer Cadets*, offering programmes in captaincy, marine engineering and radiotelegraphy operation. (Its graduates can enrol in the TEI, without examination, for up to 1 per cent of the seats available.)
- The *School for Tourist Professions (STE)*, including the Hotel and Restaurant Department, the Catering Department and the Hotel Client Account Management Department.
- The *Ecclesiastical Lykeio*, which prepares boys for the priesthood.
- The *Military School for Permanent Noncommissioned Officers (SMY)*, with sections for the army, the navy and the airforce as well as similar institutions for the police and the harbour police-coastguard.
- Various private Technical and Vocational *Lykeia*, which offer a wide range of programmes (from aircraft mechanics to paramedics).

Overall assessment. Between 1983 and 1989 the proportion of 14–18 year olds staying on at school increased by 9 per cent, reaching 80 per cent of the population of that age, the sixth highest in the EC.

All types of diploma from a *Lykeio* (that is, an *Apolyterio* from any institution, public or private, that operates as a *Lykeio*) carry the same legal value. Nevertheless, each type – apart from its perceived status – offers its holder different opportunities and qualifications. TEL graduates, in theory, enjoy most scope. They can continue their studies in tertiary education or join the labour market after vocational training. In contrast, General *Lykeio* graduates are only prepared for a seat in tertiary education, whilst apprentices and TES graduates are trained for a job.

In practice the situation is far less promising. The vocational training of all secondary education graduates is mainly academic, with no on-the-job experience. Moreover, TEL graduates receive no official recognition of their specialization. As far as General *Lykeio* graduates are concerned, they lack any form of vocational education. On the other hand, an OAED apprenticeship is the only reliable alternative for a youngster not aiming at higher education, offering its students training, job experience and income. In practice, however, the OAED training scheme is fraught with problems. Demand for training positions is high and the availability limited. Most placements are in small companies or workshops where training is unsystematic and unsupervised. The shortage of places leads apprentices to accept anything on offer, even when the type of training is unsuited to their theoretical background or interests. Their instructors are experienced workers with no special training or qualifications for the role of mentor to young people. Nevertheless, the specialized training that the apprenticeship provides, coupled with some job experience, makes it highly attractive to youngsters seeking entry to a profession, even though – in most cases – it leads to no formal recognition or accreditation. And the lack of any better trained personnel makes demand for apprenticeship graduates high among employers.

There is no list of officially recognized professions and the level of qualifications required for each. As a result, graduation from an institution of secondary technical and vocational education may not constitute (for professions where the entry requirements are laid down by statute) adequate qualification for the practice of a profession. In some cases, for example, a pass in an examination administered by the Ministry of Industry may be required.

In general, technical and vocational education has never been viewed with much enthusiasm by parents or students. For decades the educational system (with a predominantly classical and humanistic curriculum) has concentrated on preparing students for highly regarded university degrees rather than for vocationally orientated qualifications. Under the circumstances, manual labour and vocational education have traditionally been viewed as inferior to intellectual work and academic studies. This prejudice is best reflected in the number of registered students in each type of *Lykeio*: around 74 per cent of students in post-*Gymnasium* secondary education attend General *Lykeio*, 20 per cent TEL and only 4 per cent TES.

Various governments since 1974 have tried to alter the situation, creating new and more attractive types of institutions of vocational education and training. In one such attempt, in 1984, the socialist PASOK government established the EPLs. In 1992 the conservative New Democracy government introduced a new legal framework for a National System of Vocational Education and Training (see below).

Higher education

Higher education is under state control, in accordance with the Greek constitution. It is provided by the university-level institutions of higher education (*Anotata Ekpedevtika Idrymata*, AEI) and by the Technological Educational Institutions (*Technologika Ekpedevtika Idrymata*, TEI). There has been considerable growth in the proportion of young people receiving higher education, from 9 per cent of the relevant age group in 1970-1 to around 17 per cent in 1986-7. The level of participation is higher than in the Netherlands or Italy and about double that in the UK.

AEIs include seventeen universities (*Panepistimia*) and technical universities (*Polytechnia*) as well as two Highest Schools of Fine Arts (ASKT). At universities courses last a minimum of four years (eight semesters). In engineering, agriculture, veterinary medicine and dentistry the duration of studies is five years (ten semesters), six years (twelve semesters) in medicine. University graduates receive a *Ptychio* (the equivalent of a BA or BSc) and technical university graduates a diploma (BSc). In all technical universities and in several other colleges a thesis (*Diplomatiki*, diploma thesis, or *Ptychiaki*, *ptychio* thesis) is required for graduation.

University studies are mainly of an academic nature. However, there is student demand for industrial placements during the summer vacations, depending on the discipline, and an increasing number of companies provide opportunities. Placements also afford students a chance to work on their theses in an industrial context.

University graduates with a vocationally relevant degree can practise their profession after registering with the appropriate professional body (e.g. holders of engineering diplomas with the Technical Chamber of Greece (TEE); law degree holders with the local section of the Bar Association, etc.).

TEI train 'technologists' at the level of advanced vocational training. Courses last three or four years (six to eight semesters, including eight months' obligatory practical training and a graduation project). Graduates are awarded a *Ptychio* (rated above the BTEC Higher National Diploma). However, TEI graduates enjoy no professional recognition in law, and often their qualifications overlap with those of university graduates.

This situation is a result, *inter alia*, of the policies of various conservative and socialist governments which have viewed the creation of institutions of higher education as a way of meeting public demand for university-level education (or at least something close to it) as well as a means of promoting regional development. Hence, universities, faculties and departments have been established all over Greece, accepting thousands of students each year, often with little relation to local or national labour market requirements.

Postgraduate studies. Postgraduate studies are in their infancy. There is no organized system on a nation-wide basis (at least, nothing comparable with European or American standards). The very few master's programmes that exist are organized at a university-specific level. They last from one to three years and lead to a 'Diploma in Postgraduate Specialization'. More often, however, individual departments offer examinations for 'Special Postgraduate Scholars' (EMY). Selection is through competitive tests on a few relevant subjects and on a major foreign language. Successful students assist their academic advisers in teaching while studying for their PhD. EMYs receive a monthly stipend.

The *Mediterranean Agronomic Institute of Chania (MAICH)* is an independent centre for postgraduate studies and is one of the four institutions of the International Centre of Higher Mediterranean Agronomic Studies (CIHEAM). Subjects are taught in English. Studies lead to a one-year postgraduate diploma and – upon continuation for a second dear – to an MSc.

Nevertheless, postgraduate studies share the general weaknesses of undergraduate-level education. Libraries and laboratories are often poorly equipped and staffed; the inadequacy of resources is reflected in the fact that the EMY grant is less than the national minimum wage for unskilled manual workers.

Other institutions of tertiary education. Several public and private institutions – including some foreign ones – offer courses at tertiary level, mostly related to specific professions. Some claim to offer university-level education. Their qualifications, however, are not recognized officially, since, according to the Greek constitution, universities are under state control. Officially, all kinds of private institutions at the tertiary level can operate only as 'workshops of freelance studies' and award their students only certificates of attendance.

The question of private universities became highly political and polarized after the electoral victory of the New Democracy party in

1990. A commitment to the establishment of private universities was included in its manifesto. Soon after it came to power, institutions calling themselves 'colleges' and claiming to offer university-level education were established. Many advertised exclusive partnerships with foreign universities where their students could continue their undergraduate or postgraduate studies. The situation led to a public prosecutor's investigation and charges of fraud were brought against some institutions. In an attempt to clarify the situation the government introduced the legal framework for a National System of Vocational Education and Training.

Vocational training

The new legal framework

Law 2009/1992 on the National System of Vocational Education and Training is the most recent attempt to provide a national system of vocational education and training as well as a unified national system of officially recognized professional and vocational qualifications.

The law established a supervisory body, the Organization of Vocational Education and Training (OEEK). In addition to senior civil servants, its executive board includes representatives of employer and employee organizations. Education and training are provided by the Institutes of Vocational Training (IEKs), officially in operation from 1 February 1993. IEKs can be public or private institutions and are accountable to the OEEK. The OEEK itself is financed from state and EC funds, student fees to IEKs, examination fees, fees for establishing IEKs or recognizing vocational qualifications, and revenue from its own programmes.

The law also provides for a national system of professional and vocational qualifications:

- *Certificate of vocational education at level 1* for adult Gymnasio graduates after training of at least one year in an IEK.
- *Degree of vocational education and training at level 2* for Technical Vocational School (TES) graduates.
- *Degree of vocational education at level 3* for graduates of a Technical-Vocational Lykeio (TEL) and graduates of a specialization department of an Integrated Comprehensive Lykeio (EPL).

- *Diploma of vocational training at a level of post-secondary vocational training* for:

(a) Graduates of a specialization department of an Integrated Comprehensive *Lykeio* (EPL) after training of one semester in an IEK.
(b) *Ptychio* holders of a Technical-Vocational *Lykeio* (TEL graduates with a specialization degree) after training of one year in an IEK.
(c) Graduates of an EPL or of a TEL who in their third year attended stream subjects (EPL or TEL graduates with no specialization), after training of up to a year and a half in an IEK.
(d) Graduates of a General *Lykeio* or of an EPL who in their third year attended stream subjects, after training of up to two and a half years in an IEK.
(e) Holders of a level 2 degree of vocational education and training after suitable training.

Nevertheless, many important matters (such as a list of officially recognized professions with the level of qualifications required for each) have to be regulated through presidential or ministerial decrees and decisions of the executive board of the newly established OEEK.

Institutions providing vocational training

While the outcome of the above legislation has yet to be seen, in recent years increased financing from EC funds has led to a mosaic of agencies and organizations ranging from local authorities to private schools and governmental organizations offering a wide range of training programmes. The most important are as follows.

ELKEPA (Greek Productivity Centre) offers a broad spectrum of specialized short (twenty to fifty hours) and long-term (100–800 hours) training programmes and seminars ranging from management and personal development to finance and accounting. Participants range from senior executives to unemployed university graduates. Training programmes are available through the centre's Institute of Management and Institute of Information Science. It also runs in-house seminars customized to company requirements. The cost is borne by the individuals attending the programmes, their companies or the EC Social Fund. Attendance is certified with an unofficial diploma. ELKEPA is considered to be one of the best centres for postgraduate and, especially, managerial training in Greece.

The EEDE (Greek Association of Business Management) provides various long and short-term programmes and seminars as well as intra-company seminars mainly for higher-level management.

OAED operates an Intensive Vocational Training programme, Intra-Business Schools and Mobile Training Units as well as its initial apprenticeship programme (see above).

- The *Intensive Vocational Training* programme is designed for adults – mainly the unskilled unemployed but also employed people. Courses may last up to 200 days (for boiler fitters, for example) but are usually six to nine months. As with the apprenticeship programme, the Intensive Vocational Training programme is provided in the Technical–Vocational Centres (KETEK), with similar courses. Trainees receive remuneration and full medical and health insurance, and the training time is considered as job experience. Selection is through interviews or tests where applicable. However, completion of a programme does not automatically qualify a trainee to engage in a profession.
- *Intra-business Schools* operate within large firms, with programmes approved by the OAED and under its management. They aim at the intensive training of unemployed unskilled workers in skills which are of interest to the company as well as to the local community. The OAED also prepares the instructors – who can be employees of the companies themselves – with teaching seminars and provides payment and insurance for the participants. A substantial number of programmes have been subsidized in recent years under development law 1262/82 or through the European Social Fund.
- The three *Mobile Training Units* are provided for the training of adults in non-industrial areas with no facilities where a demand for skilled personnel arises.

EOMMEX (Hellenic Organization of Small to Medium Size Enterprises and Handicrafts) aims to meet the need for skilled labour in small-to-medium-size businesses. Among other services, it offers management and innovation seminars to small manufacturers and general handicraft, carpet-making, woodwork, weaving and ceramic art seminars to craftsmen. The length of the seminars varies from short (twenty-four to seventy-five hours) to long (three years in the case of carpet-making and woodwork). Programmes are carried out in the organization's workshops and instructors are the organization's personnel or invited specialist speakers.

Skilled labour and vocational training

Despite considerable improvements since the early 1960s the educational level of the labour force remains low. In 1981 57 per cent of the work force had only completed elementary school, 18 per cent the older intermediate cycle and only 8 per cent had completed higher secondary school. According to 1988 statistics, 16·5 per cent of the work force had not completed their elementary education and 4 per cent were totally illiterate. The same research argued that in the same year – according to UNESCO's definition – 20 per cent of the labour force were illiterate, and about 80 per cent 'technically illiterate' (no familiarity with technology or 'no technical culture').

This situation can be explained partly by the fact that the vast bulk of the trained work force acquired its skills through work experience, without any grounding in theoretical knowledge. An EC study of western Greece found that small and medium-sized firms in the high-technology sector experienced severe shortages of clerical, marketing and skilled manual personnel. In spring 1989 less than 2 per cent of the 25–49 year old adults (the lowest rate in the EC) had received employment-related training during the previous four weeks.

Employers and vocational training

On-the-job training for young people other than those on an OAED apprenticeship and TES, TEI and Technical University students (see earlier) is practically non-existent. Employers have to rely almost entirely on in-house training to meet their requirements. Moreover, there seems to be general mistrust by employers of the qualifications offered by the graduates of vocational education institutions. It stems from the belief that graduates have no real familiarity with industry and no practical experience and that their theoretical knowledge is out-of-date, and largely irrelevant to the real production process. The roots of this mistrust lie in the weaknesses of the educational system itself. After decades of emphasis on the classical-humanist tradition the system still suffers from its isolation from the economic and social environment.

On the other hand, firms themselves have often appeared to display little interest in fostering vocational training. While they may express strong interest in the training their staff have received, their own involvement is minimal. Rather than making use of the skills of trained staff, their prime concern frequently appears to be adapting graduates to existing tasks and routines. The problem is especially acute in small, family businesses, the vast majority.

Nevertheless, some signs of improvement can be discerned. Employers, mainly in large export-orientated companies, have shown a marked interest in establishing and running their own programmes of training and retraining, supported where appropriate by EC funds. The textile and clothing industries and some parts of the metalworking sector, in particular, have been involved in such programmes.

Management training

The educational path for future senior managers, especially in international companies, typically entails a first degree in a technical subject at a Greek university followed by a second, business or technical, qualification at a foreign university. As noted in *Recruitment* in this series, the tendency for Greek graduates to study or work for part of their early life abroad, often in North America, the UK or Germany, has created a pool of qualified managers with foreign-language skills and international experience. Graduates in accountancy and finance must have a Greek qualification and be registered with the national professional association. There are well regarded business faculties in the Universities of Athens, Piraeus and Thessalonika.

Degree subjects tend to be directly relevant to career choice. In the past it was felt that many students who did not undertake further study abroad, especially arts graduates, aspired mainly to a job in the public sector. Cuts in public spending and privatization have rendered this a difficult and unrealistic choice in the 1990s, and such graduates may now be more willing to consider work in commerce or industry.

Trade unions and vocational training

Until recently trade unions were almost wholly concerned with wage bargaining and have shown no great interest in, nor developed any strategy for, training issues. The situation has improved considerably since the establishment of the Institute of Labour (INE) by the GSEE trade union federation (General Confederation of the Workers of Greece). The INE provides support and supervision for all EC programmes in which unions are involved. The GSEE itself participates in several Community programmes for intra-company training, retraining unemployed workers, training in new technologies, training trainers, and retraining unemployed women. Costs are covered by EC funds (up to 70 per cent of the total cost of each programme) and from the GSEE's own resources. A similar increasing interest in vocational training is being expressed by local labour centres and federations. In 1992 60 per cent of these second-tier unions applied for places in retraining programmes (see *Industrial Relations* in this series). Again the costs are met jointly from EC funds (up to 60 per cent) and from the unions. The 1991 national collective agreement, in a landmark development, established a scheme under which the employers' organizations agreed to administer jointly with the GSEE the 0.45 per cent of the employers' social security contributions earmarked for vocational training and development. The GSEE is also pressing for the ratification of ILO Convention 140 on paid leave for training.

Appendix 5.1 Organizations

OAED:
Directorate of International Affairs
8 Thrakis Street
166 10 Athens
tel. + 30 1 994 2461
(for all intra-business training
programmes, funded by the EC)

INE – GSEE:
c/o Mr Vassilis Papadogamvros
27 Pipinou and Patision Streets
112 51 Athens
or PO box 3626
102 10 Athens
tel. + 30 1 883 4611–15

Pedagogical Institute:
Ministry of National Education
396 Mesogeion Street
Athens

ELKEPA:
28 Kapodistriou Street
106 82 Athens
tel. + 30 1 360 0411–7
fax + 30 1 364 0709

Chapter 6

The Irish Republic

The voluntarist principle which informs the system of industrial relations in Ireland broadly extends to training. There is an absence of any strict legislative framework governing initial and continuing training. Apart from the payment of an apprenticeship levy, employers are not obliged by law to spend any money on training employees. Although the system of higher education is regarded as producing generally high-quality graduates – if with less industrial experience than their continental European counterparts – initial and continuing training has recently come in for considerable criticism, and proposals have been made to intensify and standardize the national training effort.

These criticisms have been become especially acute in view of the relative youth of the population – some 50 per cent of citizens are aged under 25 – and continuing high levels of unemployment, particularly among school leavers coming on to the labour market with no formal qualifications. The outflow of graduates, as well as of less qualified workers, has remained high but emigration as a safety-valve could be blocked by the lull in recruitment elsewhere in Europe.

The education system

Secondary education

Secondary school education begins at the age of 12. There are two types of school: secondary schools and comprehensive or community schools. Both types are state-funded, but secondary schools are privately owned, usually by the church. Comprehensive and community schools are state-funded and state-owned.

Secondary education, which is compulsory to the age of 15, is split into two grades: the junior cycle lasts three years and leads to the Junior Certificate; the senior cycle, lasting a further two years and leading to the Leaving Certificate, takes in a broad range of up to eight subjects, usually at the age of 17–18. In order to gain entry into a higher education establishment, a school leaver must obtain a certain number of points in the Leaving Certificate, the precise number required depending on the higher education establishment applied to. In 1991 45,000 school leavers obtained the Leaving Certificate, 10,000 attempted but failed it, 12,000 gained the junior certificate and 5,000 left without gaining any qualification.

Those who leave school after having gained a Junior Certificate can opt to attend an FAS, CERT or Teagasc vocational training course (see below) or sign up for an apprenticeship scheme (see below). Those who leave school with a Leaving Certificate can either opt to apply for a place at a university or technical college or attend a post-Leaving Certificate course (PLC), covering a variety of vocations.

In 1991 a Department of Labour survey of school leavers showed that one year later 37 per cent were in employment, 36 per cent were engaged in further education, 17 per cent were unemployed, 8 per cent had emigrated and 2 per cent were not available for work. Compared with figures for the previous year, this shows an increase in the number out of work and a significant decline, for the first time in eight years, in emigration. Unemployment is lowest for Leaving Certificate students (12 per cent), rising for those with the Junior Certificate (31 per cent) and at its highest for those leaving school with no qualifications (53 per cent).

Tertiary education

Institutions. There are a number of types of higher education establishment, largely state-funded. They range from universities to technical colleges, colleges of further education and specialist institutes.

The National University of Ireland has constituent colleges in Dublin, Cork and Galway. Dublin University has one constituent college, Trinity College, Dublin. In addition, there are Dublin City University and the University of Limerick.

The Dublin Institute of Technology (DIT) together with a number of Regional Technical Colleges (RTCs) offer vocational and technical courses, some leading to degrees, which can be attended on either a full-time or a part-time basis. The DIT and RTCs receive substantial financial assistance from the European Social Fund. According to a study carried out by the European Centre for the Development of Vocational Training (CEDEFOP), some 26,000 students attended universities in

1986, 6,000 attended other higher education establishments, almost 8,000 attended vocational technical colleges, 11,000 attended regional technical colleges, 2,000 went into teacher training and 1,600 attended other colleges, including religious establishments.

Most higher education is concentrated around the cities of Dublin, Cork, Galway and Limerick, with very little education offered by third-level centres beyond those areas.

Take-up. Higher education establishments operate a selective admission system, based on offers according to the number of points obtained in the school Leaving Certificate. Applications to these establishments are co-ordinated by a centralized body, the Central Applications Office (CAO). In 1991, out of 52,000 applicants to higher education, 12,000 failed to obtain the number of points required for entry into higher education.

According to OECD figures for 1988, the proportion of students taking engineering and science degrees was fairly high by international standards, totalling 27 per cent of all degrees awarded (compared with 13–16 per cent in southern Europe, 17–19 per cent in North America, 29 per cent in Germany and 39 per cent in France). Drop-out rates are regarded as low, a feature attributable to more stringent pre-entry selection, as in the UK.

The first bachelor's degree is taken in most arts subjects after three years, and in engineering and science after four years. (All Trinity College, Dublin, bachelors' degrees are taken after four years.)

Postgraduate studies. A variety of postgraduate courses are available to students who have obtained a first degree. They may be either primarily research degrees (doctorates) or a combination of research and teaching – the case with many MAs. As well as advanced study in traditional disciplines, MAs, lasting one or two years, may also offer more vocationally orientated specialization. Universities and colleges also offer a number of one-year postgraduate diplomas in a variety of subjects.

Vocational training

Legislative framework

Industrial training. The only areas of training covered by legislation are industrial training and apprenticeship (see below). The Industrial Training Act, 1967, established the Industrial Training Authority, AnCO, now replaced by FAS (An Foras Aiseanna Saothair) under the Labour Services Act, 1987 (see below), and is concerned to provide and promote training in all industrial activities, including state industrial organizations. Under the Act, the state training body may require a particular industry to establish an Industrial Training Committee, made up of employer and employee representatives, to oversee training measures within that industry. The committee will have the power to impose a levy on employers within that industry to finance training measures. Employers may appeal to the Levy Appeals Tribunal against the levy, which may be restricted to certain types of employer. The tribunal's decision is final. This levy scheme may be altered as a result of proposals currently under discussion (see below).

Labour Services Act, 1987. This Act transferred the duties of AnCO, the former state training body, to FAS, the new state training body. The main functions of FAS are described by the Act as:

- To co-ordinate and encourage training and retraining.
- To co-ordinate specific employment schemes and work experience programmes.
- To help find employment for the unemployed, both in Ireland and within the EC.
- To liaise between employers seeking employees and prospective employees.
- To provide advisory services relating to employment and careers.

FAS will also provide private services on an individual basis.

Organizations

The main state training and employment authority is FAS. FAS administers apprenticeship training schemes (see below), offers a variety of work experience and reinsertion courses to the unemployed as well as consultancy services to the Industrial Development Authority (IDA). FAS is funded by means of a state grant and a statutory levy on employers. In March 1992 a total of 31,160 people were participating in FAS schemes, ranging from specific skill training for company employees to assistance programmes for the long-term unemployed.

The body for agricultural training is Teagasc, funded by the state (75 per cent) with assistance from the European Social Fund (25 per cent). Teagasc offers short specialist courses as well as courses leading to the Certificate in Farming and courses for young people without experience in conjunction with the Farm Apprenticeship Board.

CERT is the Council for Education, Recruitment and Training for the hotel, catering and tourism industry. It provides short-term courses, usually of thirteen weeks' duration full-time, for young people wishing to enter the profession. It also provides skill update courses for those already in employment and wishing to move to supervisory level. CERT organizes courses for the long-term unemployed of twenty-six weeks for a multi-skilled course or twenty weeks for a single discipline, in addition to six-week courses for people wishing to return to catering. It is funded mainly by the European Social Fund, the Youth Employment Levy and a grant from the hotel, catering and tourism industry. CERT also organizes external courses offering continuing training for all categories of employee, including managers and supervisors.

The National Rehabilitation Board (NRB) co-ordinates the rehabilitation and training of disabled persons. It trains disabled people with a view to their working either in companies alongside able-bodied employees, or in special organizations, either in a skilled or in an unskilled capacity. The NRB is financed jointly by the European Social Fund and the Irish state; it trained some 5,500 disabled people in 1987.

Apprenticeships

Following the Labour Services Act, 1987 (see above), AnCO's role in overseeing the apprenticeship system was taken over by FAS. FAS co-ordinates and accredits apprenticeship training courses, and accredits qualifications on completion. The qualification awarded on completion of an apprenticeship is the National Craft Certificate. Employers must notify FAS within two weeks of hiring apprentices or terminating their contract and in some industries may be required to keep a record of all apprenticeship contracts if so required by FAS. Time spent on courses away from the workplace must be counted as working time and paid accordingly. There are currently around twenty trades which are designated for apprenticeship training.

Proposals for reform. The apprenticeship system has remained largely unchanged for over twenty years. In 1986 the government issued a White Paper on manpower policy, criticizing the apprenticeship system as 'costly, inflexible and inefficient'. It suggested reducing the cost of apprenticeship to the state (which bears over half the costs of training), matching the supply of apprentices to demand and basing apprenticeship on standards achieved rather than length of time served. FAS issued a discussion document at the end of 1989 containing a number of suggestions for the improvement and development of the system.

Under the current system there is no standardized level of competence which an apprentice must attain in order to function as a craft worker. Some trained apprentices will have the National Craft Certificate, whilst others may be awarded different qualifications on completion of training. FAS has proposed the introduction of a new standards-based system of qualifications for apprenticeship, advocating a single system leading to the award of the National Craft Certificate, without which a person would not be recognized as a trained craft worker. The training would be broadly based initially, with the apprentice being able to develop specialist skills further into the apprenticeship, thereby increasing flexibility, allowing for cross-skilling and updating of skills in line with technological change. Training would take the form of a series of on- and off-the-job modules, with the length of the apprenticeship determined by the amount of time it took to pass the modules and the particular industry concerned.

There is no standardized recruitment system for apprentices, with schemes not necessarily finding the best potential apprentices. FAS proposes standardization of recruitment. Entrants should:

- Be over 16 years old.
- Have obtained a certain number of grades in their intermediate school certificate, preferably with a technical subject.
- Have passed an aptitude test.

Currently some 1,000 apprentices are taken on each year directly by employers following employers' own criteria. FAS proposes that entrants should either be screened directly by FAS or proposed by companies and subsequently screened by FAS. There would be special provisions to encourage the recruitment of certain groups, such as mature applicants (no maximum age), disabled persons and women, with a target of 10 per cent of apprenticeship places to be made available to female apprentices.

FAS also proposes the creation of a National Apprenticeship Committee to advise FAS on general provisions relating to apprenticeship, such as regional quotas, content, standards and general policy. The committee's immediate tasks would be to oversee the transition to a standards-based system, draw up recruitment guidelines and oversee the entry of special groups to apprenticeship schemes.

Off-the-job training would take place either at FAS centres or at FAS-approved training centres, vocational schools and colleges.

FAS is planning to increase the number of designated trades for apprenticeship from around twenty to forty over the coming years, alongside an increase in the total number of apprentices from the current 3,000 to 6,000. FAS eventually aims to train around 10,000 apprentices annually. New trades to be designated for apprenticeship include new technology areas such as computing and electronics.

These proposals were reinforced in a clause of the national pay agreement, signed at the beginning of 1991 for three years, the Programme for Economic and Social Progress (PESP). The clause also suggested that advisory committees containing representatives from the main employers' federation, the FIE, the construction industry employers' federation, the CIF, and the main trade union confederation, ICTU, should be set up to oversee the implementation of the proposals. Discussions are continuing between the social partners but no firm agreement on apprenticeship overhaul has yet been reached.

Funding. In spring 1992 an agreement was reached by the PESP Central Review Committee to fund apprenticeship training by means of a new levy on industrial employers of 0·25 per cent of the wage bill, after initial FAS proposals of a 0·5 per cent levy. Subject to government approval, the new levy will be introduced on 6 April 1993, payable to FAS. Additional funding will be provided by the state and by the European Social Fund, which will contribute 65 per cent of total costs. This is generally thought to be a fairer system of funding, as the spread of firms levied will be widened to all industrial employers, all paying a smaller sum than the 1·25 per cent levy previously required by FAS. The burden on the Exchequer will also be reduced, thus reducing the cost of apprenticeship training to the state and making apprenticeship more industry-based, with employers paying into funds which will be used for their particular industry.

Other initial training: post-school Leaving Certificate courses

If a school leaver has obtained the Leaving Certificate but does not wish to apply to universities or higher education colleges, there are a number of alternative vocational courses available. These are post-Leaving Certificate courses (PLCs). They usually last one year, although some can be for two or three years. They offer a variety of technical and vocational subjects, with an estimated 15,000 places on offer for entry in autumn 1992. PLCs are very popular, the number of places having increased twofold since the mid-1980s, with the range of courses on offer also increasing to over 500. The most widely available courses are business and secretarial.

PLCs are run by vocational colleges and lead to a variety of nationally recognized diplomas, depending on the subjects studied. In some cases the courses can be attended as foundation courses in preparation for entry to tertiary education or further vocational training at technical colleges. Information and administration of the courses are handled by regional Vocational Education Committees. Admission is by interview for applicants with certain grades in the school Leaving Certificate.

Continuing training

There is no statutory obligation for employers to provide training and no statutory right to time off for training. Employers can send their employees on a variety of training courses to enhance their existing skills or train them in new ones, provided by a variety of state and private institutions (see above). However, as the criticisms of the system set out below illustrate, continuing training is relatively neglected compared with the position in other EC member states.

Criticisms of vocational training

A number of studies, some carried out by FAS, and most recently an independent report, the Roche–Tansey report *Industrial Training in Ireland*, published in spring 1992, maintain that Irish workers do not receive adequate levels of training.

The Roche–Tansey report found that employers are reluctant to provide anything more than minimum levels of training for their work force, blue-collar and white-collar alike. The result is a generally low skill profile throughout the work force. The report found that the highest amount spent by companies on training was 3 per cent of the wage bill, with the average around 0.9 per cent. However, one-tenth of the top 1,000 companies surveyed spent nothing on training. Many companies interviewed felt that, where skill gaps did occur, the answer was the multi-skilling of technicians and craft workers rather than complete retraining or hiring workers to perform different tasks.

Half the companies interviewed said they used state services, including FAS, which was regarded by most as satisfactory. However, the role of FAS is restricted by the fact that larger firms tend to train workers in-house and smaller firms spend very little on training.

The education system provides a good number of graduate engineers and technicians, but they are felt to lack industrial experience upon graduation. The report advocates a change of emphasis from academic to vocationally orientated qualifications and courses in tertiary education establishments and vocational schools.

According to FAS studies, over 50 per cent of Irish workers receive no training at all, and the level of training has hardly risen over the past few years. Twenty per cent of the work force receive some kind of formal off-the-job training each year, and a further 20 per cent receive on-the-job training. However, most training is carried out in the public sector and in larger companies. The amount of training received also depended on sector, with over half the employees surveyed by FAS in manufacturing and construction and 65 per cent of employees in service companies receiving no formal training at all. Spending on training per employee totalled Ir£97 in 1990.

However, although training is a national discussion issue in the light of record levels of unemployment, FAS maintains that, unlike other European countries, Ireland does not particularly suffer from skill shortages. Some shortages are felt in specific areas of employment, but the numbers are not very significant, with vacancies being filled relatively quickly.

Reinsertion schemes and training for the unemployed

A number of schemes are in operation which aim to offer the unemployed a mixture of theoretical training and practical on-the-job experience.

Job training scheme

At the end of April 1990 in collaboration with the ICTU, FIE and CII, FAS introduced a pilot job training scheme for the unemployed. FAS hoped to make 10,000 places available to the unemployed who had been out of work for at least two months, with special consideration given to long-term unemployed and early school leavers. Companies had to assure FAS that they were intending to increase their employment level before being allowed to participate in the scheme. Training periods would vary from thirteen to twenty weeks, the cost of the training to be met by the employer, with 75 per cent reimbursed by FAS. Most of the money funding the project was provided by the European Social Fund. It was hoped that there would be a definite job opportunity in the placement company for the trainee at the end of the placement period.

However, it was revealed in 1992 that only forty-four trainees had been taken on as employees by companies as a result of the job training scheme. Take-up of the scheme on the part of companies was also well below target levels, according to a member survey carried out by the FIE and CII: 2,000 companies were participating, compared with target levels of 10,000. The scheme has been criticized for unnecessarily high levels of bureaucracy and not enough incentives for employers to participate. In September 1992 the government agreed to alter certain provisions of the scheme, such as dropping the requirement that trainees must be unemployed, thus allowing employers to recruit school leavers direct. The minimum duration of training has been reduced, from twenty-six to thirteen weeks. Companies may also top up the trainees' allowance in order to boost remuneration rates for trainees.

Employment Subsidy Scheme

FAS also set up the Employment Subsidy Scheme, with the aim of providing incentives for employers to expand their workforce, thereby creating jobs. Under the scheme, companies are entitled to a subsidy of Ir£2,808 for each employee recruited in addition to the number of employees or posts in existence with the company on 1 November 1991. This number is unlimited for established firms, while companies set up after that date may claim the subsidy for up to twelve new employees. New posts must be full-time, with the employer paying the normal tax and social deductions, paying the 'going rate' and complying with Employment Regulation Orders and Registered Employment

Agreements with regard to minimum terms and conditions for a particular industry. A total of only 141 new jobs had been created by these subsidies in March 1992; it is too early to say whether the scheme will be a significant aid to job creation.

Around 50 per cent of those taking part in FAS training or employment schemes in 1991 remained unemployed at the end of the training period, according to FAS. Around 34,000 people participated in training programmes and 22,000 in employment schemes. Job placement was highest – around 70 per cent – for those who had trained for specific skills, meaning that the placement rate for other programmes was much lower.

Youth Reach Programme

This scheme targets the estimated 10 per cent of school leavers who possess no formal qualifications. Participants receive a weekly allowance and attend education and training programmes for a period of up to two years. The training scheme includes periods of work placement in companies. The aim of the scheme is to place young people in employment or in a position where they are able to obtain formal academic or vocational qualifications.

Vocational Training Opportunities Scheme

These schemes are designed to provide training for the long-term unemployed. Those over 25 and who have been unemployed for a year or more are eligible to apply. Trainees receive the equivalent of unemployment benefit or unemployment assistance and attend courses in vocational training schools. Some participants may work towards the school Leaving Certificate whilst others may train for a particular skill.

In view of the high and rising levels of unemployment, the government is discussing proposals to offer vocational training to all those under 21 years of age who have been out of work for six months or more, thus extending the VTO scheme to an estimated further 7,500 people. The proposals have not yet been approved, as expansion of the VTOS would mean more tutors and extra funding, which may have to come from the EC Structural Fund.

Talks are also going on concerning the restructuring of FAS, creating within FAS a division for industry-related training and a division for all other schemes, including employment schemes for the long-term jobless. The transfer of vocational training schemes for under 18-year-olds, except apprentices, from FAS to the Department of Education is also being discussed.

Management training

As with initial training, management training has also come under critical scrutiny. The Galvin Committee report, released in 1989, highlighted a number of deficiencies in the provision of training for managers, noting that 'Expenditure in Ireland on management development is inadequate, whether measured by comparison with international practice or in relation to national needs.' According to the committee, an average of 1·4 per cent of the pay bill was devoted to management training. An FAS study also revealed that only 30 per cent of managers receive formal off-the-job training. Over 20 per cent of the country's top 1,000 companies spend nothing at all on management training.

Apart from universities offering degree courses and colleges offering business studies courses, there are three main providers of management training. These establishments offer initial training in the form of full-time courses in business management and MBAs, and continuous training in the form of short, day, part-time and evening courses.

The Irish Management Institute, an independent body, is financed by membership subscriptions, fees, grants from the Department of Labour and the European Social Fund. Its degree, diploma and certificate courses are validated and awarded by Trinity College, Dublin, where a good deal of the instruction is given. The four-year management degree programme leads to a BA in management and it also offers an MSc course in management practice and organization behaviour. Its two-year MBA course is run in conjunction with Fordham University, New York.

On-going management training offered by the IMI includes a variety of management development courses, some run continuously for a period of days or weeks and some run part-time over a variety of subjects, including marketing, finance, computing, personnel, law and languages. The IMI will also draw up management training programmes tailored to suit individual companies upon request.

The Institute of Public Administration (IPA) trains managers in local authorities and the health service in addition to managers in the civil service and state organizations, training some 5,000 in total each year.

It offers degree courses leading to a BA in public administration or health administration, general courses in a variety of subjects and individual courses tailored to a particular company's needs. Training courses vary in duration from a day to six months.

The Civil Service Training Centre offers shorter courses to managers in the civil service, averaging a duration of one week. It offers assistance on staff appraisal, staff development and language tuition in addition to general management courses.

There are also a variety of private management training companies in existence, offering management training and development on general themes or tailored to individual needs.

Appendix 6.1 Educational attainment

Level	Percentage of 25–64 age group
Primary	37
Lower secondary	25
Upper secondary	23
Higher education (non-university)	7
University	7

Source: OECD.

Appendix 6.2 Organizations

Government Department of
Education:
Marlboro Street
Dublin 1
tel: + 353 1 717101

Government Department of Labour:
Mespil Road
Dublin 4
tel. + 353 1 765861

FAS (State Training Authority):
27–33 Upper Baggot Street
Dublin 4
tel. + 353 1 685777
fax + 353 1 682691

Higher Education Authority:
21 Fitzwilliam Square
Dublin 2
tel. + 353 1 612748
fax + 353 1 610492

Irish Management Institute:
Sandyford Road
Dublin 16
tel. + 353 1 956911
fax + 353 1 955150

Chapter 7

Italy

Compared with other European Community countries, Italy still has a relatively short period of compulsory education, with the school leaving age at 14. However, this is compensated for to some degree by the large proportion of young people who transfer to the various forms of continuing schooling. The bulk of initial vocational training, including intermediate and technical skills, is provided through the state education system, with apprenticeship playing an important but subsidiary role, and primarily concentrated in small firms.

Secondary and tertiary education

Secondary education is highly centralized and is administered by the Ministry of Public Education. Approximately 5 per cent of lower secondary school students and 11 per cent of upper secondary school students are in non-state-run schools (which include those administered by local authorities as well as purely private institutions). Private schools must, however, conform to national legislation and regulations issued by the Ministry.

Education is compulsory between the ages of 6 and 14. Secondary education is divided into two cycles: lower secondary (*scuola media*), which extends to the age of 14 and is compulsory, and upper secondary. However, a large proportion of pupils continue beyond the age of 14 (see below), principally because initial vocational and technical training is provided through the state education system.

Lower secondary education

Pupils complete compulsory education in lower secondary school. These schools provide three years of free, standard comprehensive schooling to all children from the age of 11 to 14. For some years now there has been a proposal to increase the school leaving age to 16 in order to bring Italy into line with other European countries.

At the end of lower secondary schooling successful students are awarded a leaving certificate, the *Diploma di Licenza Media* and can proceed to upper secondary school. In 1990, 92 per cent of lower secondary pupils obtained the *licenza media* and 89 per cent continued on to the upper secondary school level.

Upper secondary education (including initial vocational and technical training)

There are a variety of upper secondary educational institutions providing courses lasting three, four or five years. Students may also opt for vocational training at one of the regional centres.

Academic courses, leading to university entrance, are provided by the *licei*. These are differentiated further into:

- The classical lyceum (*liceo classico*), where subjects such as Latin and Greek are included in the curriculum.
- The scientific lyceum (*liceo scientifico*), where the curriculum places greater emphasis on scientific subjects.
- The artistic lyceum (*liceo artistico*), with students specializing in artistic and technical subjects.

Courses at these schools last five years except in the case of the *liceo artistico*, where they last four years. Successful students are awarded a high school certificate (*Diploma di Maturità*). Those receiving either a classical or a scientific diploma can proceed to university, while those with a *diploma artistica* can go either to an Academy of Fine Arts or to a university faculty of architecture. Students with a *diploma artistica* wishing to enrol at other faculties must complete a further year's study.

Teacher training is undertaken by the *istituto magistrale* for primary school teachers or the *scuola magistrale* for nursery school teachers. The *istituti* provide four-year courses leading to university, while the *scuole* provide three-year courses which do not.

Technical and commercial upper secondary education providing intermediate-level skills is well developed and takes place at technical institutes (the *istituti tecnici*). It is the single most important study option at upper secondary level, with 1·3 million students in 1990–1 (see below). Most courses last five years, and just over 50 per cent of all enrolled students follow courses in commerce. The final qualification for students leaving such schools is the *Diploma di Maturità Tecnica*, which is fully recognized by employers in industry, commerce and agriculture and also entitles the holder to enter university. There is some institutional specialization, with separate *istituti* for agriculture, commerce and accountancy, business management, tourism, surveying, industrial technology, aerospace, maritime skills and home economics. (Accountancy, for example, is not primarily a graduate profession in Italy.)

The main institutional form through which initial vocational training is provided are the vocational training institutes (*istituti professionali*). These are open to students with a lower secondary school certificate or to any candidate over 14 years of age who passes an entrance examination. Successful students obtain a *Diploma di Qualifica* in the specialization taken. Courses are two to three years long and cover a variety of fields, such as industry, agriculture, crafts and trade. On completion, students are awarded a vocational skills diploma (*Diploma di Qualifica Professionale*) attesting to their skill in a particular trade and can attempt the entrance examination to one of the technical institutes to follow a course to develop their basic skills. (According to the EC's rating of comparable qualifications, the *Diploma di Qualifica* is counted as equivalent to a UK NVQ level III in engineering/metalworking, and levels 2/3 in commerce and banking.)

Some *istituti professionali* offer more specialized courses (*corsi speciali di sperimentazione*) which extend the usual three years to five, culminating in the award of a *Diploma di Maturità Professionale*. This entitles the holder to enrol at a university. There are specialized vocational institutes for agriculture, hotels and catering, industry and crafts, tourism, traditional 'female' occupations (shorthand and typing, fashion design, secretarial, graphic design, dressmaking), the food industries, woodworking (including musical instruments), maritime skills, commerce, and education for the blind.

Most vocational training is conducted on a full-time basis, and there are only a small number of pilot schemes offering work experience or placements. Some special employment/training contracts also entail a combination of instruction and work experience.

In 1990–1 the breakdown of students in upper secondary education by institution was as follows: initial vocational training, 23 per cent; technical training, 42 per cent; teacher training, 7 per cent; scientific lyceum, 15 per cent; classical lyceum, 8 per cent; linguistic lyceum, 1 per cent; artistic lyceum, 4 per cent.

Tertiary education

Access to university education is via the possession of either the school leaving certificate or a technical qualification. Admission is restricted only in a few selected institutions or for high-demand specialisms (dentistry, medicine). This very open structure, combined with fairly long courses, has produced notoriously overcrowded institutions and high drop-out rates. According to OECD figures, only just over 30 per cent of Italian students complete their degree, compared with 94 per cent in the UK.

Tertiary education takes place almost exclusively in universities (although in technical specialisms these may be termed *politecnici*). They are mainly administered by the state, with a small number in the private sector which are also largely funded by the state and obliged to conform to national regulations. While the private institutions account for only a small minority of student numbers, they include some of the most highly regarded universities, such as the Bocconi in Milan, LUISS in Rome and the Catholic universities in both those cities. Many of these institutions have developed close links with business and, unlike most state universities, frequently operate a system of selection. The Bocconi has a well regarded school of business administration (Scuola di Direzione Aziendale) offering an MBA. There are also business schools offering MBAs at the universities of Padua, Genoa, Bari and Turin. (However, the master's degree is not a recognized academic qualification in Italian law – see below.)

Enrolment for science and engineering degrees is fairly low by international standards. Sixteen per cent of all degrees awarded were in the natural sciences, engineering or maths/computing in 1988, compared with 29 per cent in Germany and 40 per cent in France.

There are three types of academic qualification, the *diploma universitario* (DU), the *diploma di laurea* and the *dottorato di ricerca*. Students not wishing to embark on a full degree course could, until a recent change, opt for a two or three-year course at a *scuola diretta a fini speciali* – a school with special aims – run by the university and leading to the *diploma* qualification. This will now be phased out (see below, 'Recent changes').

The main academic degree is the *diploma di laurea*, typically awarded after four or five years' study, depending on specialism. The qualification means passing annual examinations over the entire course as well as the submission of a thesis. Students can choose between a wide variety of major and minor options, with graduation exams taking place three times a year.

Postgraduate studies. Universities are responsible for postgraduate studies and run the *scuole di specializzazione* – specialization schools – offering courses lasting one to five years, depending on the field of study, which lead to the *diploma di specialista*.

Students wishing to further their studies in their own field rather than specialize in a new one can attend a *corso di perfezionamento* – a specialization course, lasting a maximum of one year. At the end of it they are awarded an *attestato di frequenza*, an attendance certificate.

Only since the University Reform Act, 1980, have students been formally able to pursue academic research leading to a doctoral qualification (*Dottorato di Ricerca*). Master's degrees, mainly in business studies, are awarded by some universities. Although not formally recognized in law, they are accepted by employers.

Recent changes. In 1989 the administration of the universities passed from the Ministry of Public Education (*Ministero della Pubblica Istruzione*) to the new Ministry of Universities and Scientific and Technological Research (*Ministero dell' Università e della Ricerca Scientifica e Tecnologica*), set up with the aim of co-ordinating higher education development and scientific research.

In 1990 the *Diploma Universitario* or *Laurea Breve* was introduced, a first-level degree course lasting two or three years. The change is intended to bring Italy into line with other European university systems such as those of Britain, Germany and France. It also aims to keep up with rapid technological change, particularly in engineering, economics and medicine, and to reduce the high drop-out rate among students as well as to provide more flexible courses in growing subject areas. Having achieved the *laurea breve*, students can proceed to study for the full *diploma di laurea*. The *laurea breve* means that the *scuole a fini speciali* will be phased out.

The year 1990 also saw changes in university teacher training courses for nursery and primary school teachers.

Vocational training

Despite a number of reforms introduced since the late 1970s, vocational training continues to exhibit a number of problematic features already tackled elsewhere in the EC. For example, there is no centralized system for the certification of training courses and no corresponding institutional network developing nationally accepted training standards or materials. Links between vocational training and higher education are also virtually non-existent.

Vocational training is provided in several ways, funded both by the state and privately.

The weakness of guilds or similar associations, combined with attempts to establish a national model via the state, has led to the concentration of training provision within the public education system and under the control of the state.

State provision is delivered by three institutions. The state-run technical and vocational training institutes provide initial and intermediate training, are regulated by the Ministry of Public Education and are part of the general system of education (for details see above). All costs of initial training within this system are borne by the public exchequer. In addition, there are regional training centres (*centri di formazione professionale regionale*) which are co-ordinated by the Ministry of Labour. Training provided by the regions is described below. Apprenticeship is underdeveloped, and serves mainly as a special scheme to encourage the employment of young people, with concessions on social security contributions for employers (see below).

In recent years one of the most important developments in state provision has been a pilot study, 'Project '92', which aims to reform vocational education as a first step towards reforming all secondary schooling, including raising the school leaving age to 16.

Regional centres

The regions have legal responsibility for all vocational training, though in practice it is mainly carried out within the national state system. Only 380,000 school leavers were directly attending Regional Centres (CFPs) in 1990–1, compared with 1·3 million in technical institutes. The centres train people for all three sectors of the economy – agriculture, industry and services. Courses vary considerably from region to region, and national data on provision are notoriously difficult to collect because of its fragmented nature. However, according to the official training research organization ISFOL, a good guide is to examine the types of courses planned by the centres each year, most of which actually take place. In 1990/1 the picture was as shown in table 7.1. More courses are planned for the south, compared with other regions (probably reflecting the higher rate of unemployment and underdevelopment of other training institutions), with training in service occupations dominant in all regions.

Table 7.1   Vocational training courses planned by regional centres, 1990–1

Sector	No. of courses planned	% of total
Agriculture	3,578	16.9
Industry and craft	6,520	30.8
Services	11,038	52.2

Source: ISFOL.

Students undertaking any of the basic (first and second-level) courses provided by the regional centres do not need a lower secondary school certificate (*licenza di scuola media*) unless they are planning to progress to the second level. Courses at the first level last two years, while those at the second level generally last one year. None of the courses qualifies a student upon completion to enter university. Nor do those trained at these centres enjoy the same opportunities for employment as those trained in the state vocational training institutions and technical institutes. There is pressure for reform, and it is envisaged that change can be attempted within the framework of the draft legislation to reform secondary schooling and to raise the school leaving age.

The regional centres also provide some adult vocational training, mainly aimed at the unemployed and those made redundant owing to company restructuring.

Transitional job training schemes

Various types of scheme have been developed to foster training on the job or provide a mixture of training and work experience. Such schemes can be a route into work for those without any skills, or may follow completion of initial vocational training in the public education system. The main schemes, which are administered through the regions, are as follows.

Training/employment contracts (*contratti di formazione e lavoro*, CFL) together with apprenticeship contracts (*apprendistato*) have been developed and given statutory backing to induce employers to take on and train young people. Employers are offered reduced social security contributions and are required by law to commit themselves to providing training but there are no formal systems to verify that proper training actually takes place. Employers have always tended to rely on older, more experienced workers passing on their knowledge in an informal way. For this reason unions have exerted pressure and have achieved the establishment of a small number of more formalized on-the-job training schemes. The schemes are aimed at young people with a low level of basic education.

Apprenticeships are regulated by a specific statute (law 25/1955) and are concentrated overwhelmingly in craft firms. Apprentices may be aged between 14 and 20, and are allowed to work on apprentice contracts – at special rates of pay – for up to five years. The primary criticism of apprenticeship training is the failure of the system to guarantee that apprentices attend the prescribed eight hours' school instruction intended to accompany the on-the-job element. The apprenticeship system, which nonetheless still embraces some 560,000 young people, has been perceived as losing its value as a general vocational qualification because of the lack of a systematic theoretical component.

Job retraining (*riconversione professionale*) is aimed at the unemployed, those in *cassa integrazione* (the wage fund which supplies payment to workers in companies undertaking restructuring exercises – see *Industrial Relations* in this series) and those seeking to change their occupation.

In-company and continuing training

There is no legal obligation on employers to provide training, although employees may enjoy certain statutory or agreed rights to time off for education and training (see below). Substantial differences in practice and organization are found, primarily depending on company size. Whereas training in smaller concerns is informal, and conducted without the help of an in-company training department, larger firms have training departments which in many cases have become independent organizations offering training to other firms. (Both Fiat and Olivetti established such agencies, for example.) Because a good deal of basic vocational training is provided by public bodies (see above), much company-based training is concerned with training and developing managers.

Medium-sized firms tend to provide more formalized training, often with the help of a small training department. This will usually have recourse to the outside market to provide the actual training. An exception would be firms which, although small or medium-sized, have a high level of investment in information technology and therefore more stringent training needs. Such organizations are much more likely to have a larger, more structured training department in-house.

Resort to outside providers appears to be growing, and according to a survey of consultants carried out in the mid-1980s training services accounted for just over 10 per cent of the fee income of management consultancy companies (the largest single source of income after computer consultancy). This trend is attributed both to a growing interest in in-company training (spurred on by technical change) and organizational streamlining in which more functions are subcontracted.

Some industry associations also function as external training providers to member companies, especially for the development of sectorally specific skills. One example is IFA, the National Association for Vocational Training in the Insurance Sector, which offers a broad range of courses for all skill levels for its eighty member companies. Courses include specialized programmes for brokers, general management in the industry, and foundation and induction courses for employees.

Confindustria, the national employers' organization (see appendix), also operates its own training agency, ENFAPI, which is run as an independent limited company jointly with a number of major employers (including Fiat, Pirelli, Zanussi, IBM Italia and Montedison).

Hard facts on the incidence and costs of continuing training in Italy are notoriously hard to come by, reflecting the lack of national standards and statistics in the training field beyond the public education service.

Managerial training

Most senior managers in large and medium-sized companies will be graduates. Although the large number of small firms, which play an especially important role in the Italian economy, are likely to be led by entrepreneurs (and their families), these are now also increasingly likely to be university-trained. Degrees in economics and business (*economica e commercio*) and law (*giurisprudenza*) are common for entrants into general management. Engineering graduates may also be recruited into general management as well as into technical specialisms. The Bocconi in Milan, which has its own business school, is the most prestigious university for those looking for careers in top management (see also above, 'Tertiary education').

Although MBAs are not formally recognized in Italy, some business schools offer them, and this is bolstered by institutional and many personal links with the USA. Formal management education, as well as the use of external seminars and short courses, has also been fostered by the increased demand for professional managers from medium and small companies, where attitudes to training have become much more positive in the past decade or so. In common with Germany, Italy is experiencing much greater managerial mobility than previously, both in the form of executives moving company to advance their careers and in an increased readiness by businesses to dismiss underperforming managers. Both phenomena are likely to raise demand for a transferable management qualification.

Management development is given a high priority by both large and medium-sized companies. The latter more typically use consultants as providers of training. All large firms, however, have in-house facilities for management training. Recruits into larger organizations will generally join a two-year graduate programme which combines a theoretical element with circulation through the various departments. Furthermore, whereas in the past larger firms kept to established programmes for such issues as succession planning and triennial career reviews, there is now increasing experimentation with more flexible approaches designed to foster internal entrepreneurship and the devolution of decision-making.

Employee time-off rights for further education and training

Statutory provision

The Worker's Statute of 1970 gave all employees in companies employing more than fifteen people certain rights to facilitate study. Article 10 of this law distinguishes between employees attending university (where attendance at lectures is not compulsory) and workers 'enrolled and regularly attending classes at primary, secondary or vocational schools which are public, state-approved or authorized to award legally recognized qualifications'. The latter – but not the former – are entitled to hours of work arranged to facilitate attendance at classes and preparation for examinations. In addition, they may not be compelled to work overtime or during weekly rest periods.

All employees, including university students, are entitled to paid leave in order to sit examinations.

Collective agreements

Many collective agreements contain additional provisions on study leave. The pace-setting agreement in this field was the national engineering agreement of 1973, which specified that workers wishing to attend certain schools (that is, state schools or others agreed by the employers and unions) were entitled to total paid leave of up to 150 hours over a period of three years. (This leave could be used up in one year by any individual employee.) The allowance was subsequently increased to 250 hours for workers attending primary school courses (that is, completing their basic education under the Italian system). There are certain limitations on the use of study leave under the engineering agreement:

- Student workers must produce a school certificate verifying their attendance for a number of hours two-thirds more than the number paid for by the employer.
- No more than 2 per cent of the work force may be simultaneously absent from work for study reasons.
- Absence from work for study reasons must not hamper normal production.

In addition the agreement provides for 120 hours of unpaid leave per annum for all workers, provided that it can be scheduled to take account of the company's organizational and production needs. Similar agreements exist in most sectors, although the number of hours' leave and the limitations may vary slightly from sector to sector.

Sector-level agreements along these lines are aimed at improving the educational standard of workers in general. For individual workers following courses other than the approved ones, other provisions may exist at company level or may be worked out on an informal basis.

Appendix 7.1 Organizations

Ministry of Labour and Social
Security (Ministero del Lavoro e
della Previdenza Sociale):
Via Flavia 6
00187 Roma
tel. + 39 6 4683

Ministry of Public Education
(Ministero della Pubblica Istruzione):
Viale Trastevere
00100 Roma
tel. + 39 6 58491

ISFOL
Institute of Vocational Training
(Istituto per lo Sviluppo della
Formazione Professionale dei
Lavoratori):
Via G. B. Morgagni 33
00161 Roma
tel. + 39 6 854 1744

AIDP (Italian personnel managers'
association):
Via Cornalia 19
20124 Milano
tel. + 39 2 67 09 558

Confindustria (central employers'
organization):
Viale dell'Astronomia 30
0100 Roma
tel. + 39 6 59031

Chapter 8

The Netherlands

The Netherlands has one of the most egalitarian higher education systems in Europe, with a long-standing tradition of decentralization and freedom of choice. Much of the emphasis is on providing study opportunities for all, geared to preparing the individual for a specific career. One important aspect of education in the Netherlands is that it has been traditionally established along religious lines. There is a constitutionally guaranteed freedom that education may be made available by any provider. As a consequence, private schools, which must meet a set of statutory requirements, are funded by the government according to the same criteria as state schools. In practice this means that approximately 70 per cent of all schools in the Netherlands are publicly funded but privately run. This has led to the existence of an almost bewildering variety of secondary education establishments in particular. In addition, the system has many in-built opportunities for moving from one stream to another, and for continuing into higher and further education. However, the emphasis remains very strongly on obtaining formal training and qualifications.

Following the advice of a government commission whose report was published in 1990 – the Rauwenhoff Commission – a series of educational reforms has been initiated drawing together and streamlining the majority of current laws. New legislation is expected to be finally passed by 1996. The aim is to enhance the flexibility of the system in order to allow greater movement between institutions, as well as to encourage individual flexibility and adaptability in vocational education.

Responsibility for education is divided between central, regional and local government with an increasing tendency to decentralization, including local management of schools. Central control is exerted to maintain national standards and qualifications, to stipulate minimum numbers of students, set broad curricular requirements, monitor teaching standards and allocate funds. Provision of state schools (*openbare school*) is the responsibility of the regional authorities. Increasing decentralization and greater school-level control is planned for the 1990s.

In contrast to many other European countries, where pay and career prospects for graduates can be determined by which institution a graduate has attended and the duration of their studies, the emphasis in the Netherlands is much more on market conditions and individual performance.

Much initial vocational training is provided under the state education system, with a vocationally orientated stream from age 12 and various gradations extending up to vocationally geared tertiary education. There is also a well developed apprenticeship system.

The education system

Education starts at the age of 4, although it is compulsory only from the age of 5, and continues until at least 16 years. However, there is a legal obligation for all 16–17 year old school leavers to attend part-time vocational classes for one or two days per week for a further two years.

Secondary education

Secondary education is structured into two paths: vocational and general education. A common first year of secondary education allows for some transfer between the two streams. Legislation passed in 1992 (*Wet op de basisvorming*), due to come into force in 1993, sets out to reinforce this facility by integrating the first three years of secondary education. Vocational secondary education is outlined below under 'Vocational education and training'.

General secondary education is divided into four main streams, each corresponding to a different type of school:

- *Pre-university* education (VWO, *voorbereidend wetenschappelijk onderwijs*) in a *Gymnasium* or *Atheneum* lasts six years to age 18, and is intended to prepare students for university or higher vocational colleges (HBO, see below).
- *Senior general secondary* education (HAVO, *hoger algemeen voortgezet onderwijs*), which lasts five years to the age of 17, and confers the right to enter higher vocational education (or transfer to VWO).

- *Junior general secondary* education (MAVO, *middelbaar algemeen voortgezet onderwijs*), lasting four years, to the age of 16. School pupils who obtain a certificate under MAVO can either enter the labour market direct, enter intermediate vocational education (MBO, see below) or transfer into senior general secondary education in order to gain entry to higher vocational education.

- *Junior secondary pre-vocational* education (LBO, *lager beroepsonderwijs*), which lasts four years, to the age of 16, and runs parallel to the other forms of compulsory secondary education set out above (VWO, HAVO, MAVO, etc.). Although termed 'vocational', the courses have a substantial general content, especially in the first two years, with more vocational emphasis in the latter part of the course. The numbers attending pre-vocational schools have fallen substantially in recent years, although a small rise was reported in the 1991/2 academic year. An LBO certificate permits entry to senior vocational training (MBO), a KMBO course (see below) or an apprenticeship.

In all in 1989, some 756,000 pupils were pursuing junior and senior and pre-university education, and 253,000 junior secondary vocational education.

Higher education

There are two main sectors of higher education: the universities, which offer scientific/academic education (*wetenschappelijk onderwijs*), and the higher vocational (*hoger beroepsonderwijs*, HBO) schools. (In 1989, 170,000 students were at universities and 235,000 in higher vocational education.) The two are governed by separate legislation, but efforts are being made to move to a more unified system. There are thirteen universities (three are universities of technology, one is a university of agriculture and nine are general universities) plus the Open University. Most of these are public bodies and are government-funded (up to some 80 per cent of costs), but they do not all provide the same range of courses.

In contrast to most universities, the HBOs are privately run. There are eighty-five HBO universities (*hogeschool*) and the number of students on these courses has increased markedly over the past few years, with a total of some 180,000 enrolled on over 300 courses in 1989/90.

Just short of 20 per cent of the work force (aged 25–64) currently hold a tertiary education qualification: 13 per cent from an HBO institution and 6 per cent from a university. University drop-out rates are low by international standards: 87 per cent of those who enter higher education graduate (compared with 94 per cent in the UK, 55 per cent in France and 31 per cent in Italy).

Higher education in the Netherlands aims to be open to as wide a spectrum of the population as possible, and there are no entrance exams as such to university. Entry is open to anyone holding a VWO-level school leaving certificate. This is sat after six years' secondary education, generally at the age of 18, in six subjects (Dutch and one foreign language are compulsory). A quota system may be applied on a national basis to admissions if the number of candidates exceeds the number of places available, or to limit supply if the labour market is temporarily saturated with graduates holding a particular qualification. This system has been used repeatedly for medicine, dentistry and veterinary science. Entry to the higher vocational institutions requires a HAVO-level school leaving certificate, generally in five subjects.

Since 1982 the length of basic university courses has been set at four years, although it can be extended to a maximum of six. Graduates are awarded the title *doctorandus* (Drs) – comparable to a UK master's degree – except in engineering and law, where the titles are *ingenieur* (Ir.) and *meester in de rechten* (Mr.) respectively. A limited number of students go on to obtain a research degree, *doctorate* (Dr), which takes a further four years to complete.

HBO courses last between two and four years, and typically involve a commercial or industrial placement. They lead to a bachelor's degree, after which students may be admitted to a university course for further study. (There is also a possibility of earlier transfer under certain circumstances.)

Vocational education and training

Vocational secondary education

Vocational secondary education consists of:

- Junior secondary vocational training (LBO) from the age of 12–16, as explained above.
- Senior vocational training (*middelbaar beroepsonderwijs*, MBO)

which follows from LBO or MAVO (see above) and lasts three or four years.

- A short-term MBO course (KMBO) has been available since 1979 which lasts two to three years.

Attendance on MBO and KMBO courses rose dramatically during the 1980s, and in 1989 some 490,000 students were enrolled (of whom 25,000 were on KMBO courses). Following changes in 1990 a number of MBO institutes were merged to enhance flexibility in training content and give increased autonomy to the individual establishments as regards teaching methods, staff policy and fund allocations. Almost 85 per cent of MBO establishments are privately run (26 per cent Roman Catholic, 20 per cent Protestant and 40 per cent nondenominational) with only 14 per cent directly state-operated. MBO courses are intended to provide intermediate training, with individuals advancing to lower levels of management/supervision. MBO training has four options:

- Engineering and technology, including laboratory and maritime education.
- Economics and administration, covering trade and commerce, textiles, food and catering and tourism.
- Social services and health care.
- Agriculture, including forestry and food technology.

All MBO courses include a period of practical training and/or industry placement, although its duration varies according to the course. Government funding of MBO and KMBO establishments is decided on pupil–teacher ratios and success rates.

In the past MBO and KMBO courses were criticized for being slow to adapt to new technology and changes in working practices, and for offering a limited curriculum. Since 1986 a number of amalgations and reforms of (K)MBO institutes have led to the social partners being increasingly involved in discussions on content change, funding requirements and teaching methods. The aim was, and still is, to create larger, better equipped and more autonomous institutions. By 1994 all MBO institutes will be required to have at least 600 students, although certain specialist schools will be able to obtain exemption from this regulation. In addition, no more separate KMBO institutes are to be set up. Instead all MBO schools will be required to offer a short course option. These changes resulted in a reduction of the number of old-style

(K)MBO institutes from 382 to 140 in 1991. Final examinations and qualifications are still set by the regional authorities, although schools have been given more freedom to design their own curricula.

Under legislation passed in 1989 schools and other educational establishments may provide training services to industry or companies. Educational institutions must apply to the Ministry of Education for a licence, with minimum standards and requirements to be met for courses, examinations and qualifications for entry.

Apprenticeships

As explained above, young people aged 16 who are no longer in full-time education are required to attend some form of educational or training establishment for one or two days per week. One means of complying is through an apprenticeship, which can be undertaken either in a manual craft trade or in commerce and services. Most people embarking on an apprenticeship have an LBO certificate: if it has not been obtained, the basic apprenticeship takes a year longer.

Apprenticeships are regulated by statute law (*Wet op het Leerlingwezen*), which stipulates the obligations and rights of the employer and the apprentice. Under the law, the schooling component of the apprenticeship is the responsibility of the schools, and the employer is responsible for the practical training.

Most apprenticeships consist of up to three levels. The first lasts for two or three years and includes the compulsory schooling element. This is provided by attendance at a recognized institution, where two-thirds of the time is spent on theoretical work-orientated training and one-third on more general education. This initial phase is completed by an examination for a nationally recognized initial vocational diploma (*beginnend beroepsbeoefenaar*) as a craft worker. The second level, lasting one to two years, extends the initial basic training (*volleerd beroepsbeoefenaar*), and may lead on to a third level of further specialization, lasting one year, and offering the prospect of a move into management or supervision.

Each sector of industry has a bipartite body responsible for apprenticeships; currently there are thirty-one such bodies. Among other things they are responsible for co-ordinating theoretical and on-the-job training, drawing up the general programmes for apprentices on a national basis, setting and marking examinations, and monitoring apprenticeship contracts. All these organizations are funded by the government. At the end of 1989 there were some 136,000 apprentice-ship contracts, with an increasing percentage of older apprentices (over 27 years of age).

Adult education and training for the unemployed

For a number of years there have been moves to harmonize the Netherlands' complex adult education and training systems, in particular for adults with a low level of education. In 1987 a number of legislative reforms and innovations provided for a more uniform approach with better co-ordination of planning, funding and standards control, implementing a system of formal recognition for commercial education establishments. A report, with a series of recommendations, was published in 1990 by the Advisory Commission on Education and the Labour Market (the Rauwenhoff Commission). The recommendations included the need for a more systematic approach to the organization and co-ordination of training courses, and a clearer division of responsibilities, as well as a need to work more closely with business. In the wake of this report a number of legislative reforms were initiated and earlier proposals were implemented. The most important of these were the Adult Education Act (*Kaderwet Volwasseneneducatie*), 1991, and the Law on Short-term Vocational Training (*Wet op het Cursorisch Beroepsonderwijs*), coming into force in August 1993, which is essentially a framework law drawing together much of the existing education and vocational training legislation. The intention is that twenty-eight regional service centres, linked closely with the twenty-eight employment services (see below), will then merge with a number of career advice centres and become responsible for overseeing educational and training organizations. Although a number of laws have yet to come into force, many of the provisions have already been put in place and are, at least in part, operational.

Under the Employment Act (*Arbeidsvoorzieningswet*), 1991, the Central Employment Service (Centraal Bestuur Arbeidsvoorziening, CBA) of the Ministry of Labour and Social Security, which is responsible for vocational training and development schemes for the unemployed, was hived off from the Ministry itself. This was partly a response to calls from the social partners and a recommendation from the Social and Economic Council (SER) that certain issues, notably training, should be the joint responsibility of employers, unions and government. The CBA draws up multi-year policy programmes for implementation by its twenty-eight regional services, which determine the number of unemployed to be trained and the appropriate educational requirements. A number of training institutions fall under the control of the CBA: the Vocational Training Centres (*Centra voor Vakopleiding*, CV) and the Centres for Job Orientation and Preparation (*Centra voor Beroepsorientatie en Beroepsoefening*, CBB). As the number of places available at these centres is relatively limited, other educational establishments are able to compete for CBA training contracts (see above).

At a CV the courses offered are usually short-term – on average seven months – and cover technical and administrative subjects. There are twenty-one technical and eleven administrative centres. All CV training is very practically orientated, and aimed primarily at the unemployed. Some 20,000 participants are involved each year, although only 7,900 places are available for the theoretical aspects of the training at the centres themselves. The CBB courses target the groups most 'at risk' in the labour market such as the long-term unemployed and those with a low level of formal qualifications or none.

Under the auspices of the FNV trade union women's organization, the Vrouwenbond, a number of women's training centres have been set up. These are for women over 25 years of age with minimal or no qualifications who have not yet been in employment or who wish to return to employment after a significant period of absence. Training programmes are often part-time and are specifically designed to suit women with school-age children. The courses last between one and two years and specialize particularly in computer studies. There are nine centres with a total of 1,000 places available. Six of them are fully subsidized by the regional services of the CBA, the other three also receive some municipal funding. The success rate, measured by the percentage of those who obtain full-time employment upon completion of the course, is relatively high, averaging 70–80 per cent.

As part of the measures to improve the opportunities of job seekers and increase the number of apprenticeships, the law on youth training was amended in 1990 (*Bijdrageregeling Vakopleiding Leerlingwezen*, BVL). Among the changes were the abolition of the upper age limit on apprentices, which had been set at 27 years. The BVL provides for a number of government subsidies which are paid either into sectoral training funds and distributed according to programmes drawn up by the funds themselves, or into joint training funds for several companies which co-operate in practical training programmes. This is termed *Gemeenschappelijke Opleidingsactiviteit* (GAO). In both instances the funds are controlled jointly by unions and employers. Additional subsidies are available to further the intake of women into traditionally male occupations and to encourage ethnic minorities and/or the disabled. The law requires that at least fifteen hours per week must be devoted to practical training, and that a specific policy plan should be submitted in cases where the additional subsidy is to be paid, detailing measures to stimulate the intake of the target groups. The basic BVL subsidy was NFl 3,500 (£1,130) in 1990, although it was reduced slightly in 1991/2. Further sectoral training programmes for the unemployed registered at unemployment offices are available in small and medium-sized companies. Again, these programmes are drawn up and implemented by representatives of employees and employers, on a regional basis. Subsidies cover all training costs up to a maximum of NFl 10,000 (£3,225) per place.

Continuing training and retraining

Although the Dutch system of vocational education, principally the various MBO options, is broadly based and offers formal training to a large number of young people, it suffers from disadvantages which employers must offset through in-house provision. In the first place, people who complete standard vocational education are often aged at least 21 when they are ready to enter employment but still lack industrial experience or functional knowledge. However, the breadth of vocational education means that often only a short period of company training is needed to allow the employee to become productive. This breadth of employment also allows for subsequent mobility within the firm, often with no further training or at least with only short in-service courses. The company training effort appears to be substantial: according to a CEDEFOP study carried out in the mid-1980s, about one in four employees had some form of training over a one-year period. Whereas larger firms (500+ employees) tend to have in-house facilities, smaller firms either share training or use external providers.

No conditions are placed on the development, operation or context of company training schemes carried out in-house. Nor do trainers have to be qualified teachers, as distinct from apprenticeship training, where instructors are qualified in their particular field of instruction.

Retraining for employees and further training options have become increasingly common features of collective agreements over the past five years, with some form of educational and training measures included in agreements covering some 80 per cent of the total number of employees affected by collective agreements. The scope of employee training has also increased, with a corresponding rise in the number of external organizations offering training courses. A Central Bureau of Statistics survey carried out in 1987 showed that 60 per cent of companies have some form of in-house training, mostly short courses lasting five days or less.

Management training

A large proportion of Dutch managers hold university or HBO qualifications. Although the subject pursued at tertiary level is more relevant to subsequent career choice than in the UK, there is some degree of flexibility, and arts graduates, for example, may be drawn into general graduate trainee programmes or may convert to business studies. There is a difference between large and small firms; the latter have difficulty retaining graduates, and more of their managers are developed from skilled workers and specialists. Both the MBO and apprenticeships have scope for training in aspects of supervision.

MBAs have become popular, being offered by some universities and private colleges, often with links with US institutions. Their perceived value varies considerably. The MBA offered by the Rotterdam School of Management (Erasmus University) is particularly well regarded.

Time-off rights and agreed provisions

Educational and training leave is not covered by law, other than for young people who have not completed the legal requirement of ten years' full-time education. Employers are obliged to agree to release such employees to attend training for the required number of hours per week (see above).

Additional educational leave, primarily for young workers, is provided for in collective agreements. The 1992 textile industry collective agreement, for example, established a commission for education and training to oversee and develop vocational training within the industry.

Employers are obliged to allow employees under the age of 18 who have already completed their ten years' compulsory education to take a maximum of one whole or two half days' paid leave per week to participate in vocational training courses linked with their employment. The Hoechst collective agreement enables employees under 19 years of age to follow vocational training courses for one whole or two half days, and where employees are on evening courses for three evenings per week or more they may be entitled to a half day's leave per week. A number of collective agreements also have separate training and employment creation programmes, detailing what types of course are available for vocational training.

A survey carried out by the Ministry of Labour's collective agreement monitoring service, the DCA, for 1991/2 showed that 144 collective agreements contained training clauses and that approximately 372 specific training-related agreements had been signed in 1992. Whereas the majority dealt with general schooling requirements in the period 1990/1, the DCA found that the 1992 agreements had a greater emphasis on employment creation, training and development. Many agreements provide specific leave for special groups of employees, such as young people, or older employees in need of retraining.

Funding

There is no legislation regulating the division of funding for education and training, and it is therefore an on-going matter for discussion. However, the constitution allows any person the freedom to provide education as long as a certain number of criteria and standards are met, which in practice means that the government funds almost all compulsory education (up to the age of 16). Most funding is channelled through the Ministry of Education and Science, with the Ministry of Social Affairs responsible for certain educational initiatives in the context of labour market policies. Some health care courses are funded by the Ministry of Health. Higher education and part time education after 16 years of age may require some financial contribution from students and/or parents, with loans and some grants available for most students.

The budget for the Ministry of Education for 1992 totalled NFl 31 billion (£10·3 billion). Some NFl 2·8 billion – about 8·5 per cent – is devoted to adult education and vocational training, and NFl 1,800 million to higher vocational training. In addition, the Ministry of Agriculture allocates NFl 1,000 million (£320 million) to education, and the Ministry of Social Affairs a further NFl 1,300 million (£410 million).

An agreement was signed between the social partners and the government in 1991 for government funding of vocational training in the period 1991–4. The agreement stipulates that finance for MBO education and apprenticeship schemes is to be assessed in relation to the costs of HAVO and VWO secondary education (see above).

The latest figures show that about 3 per cent of the wage bill was spent by companies (including organizations in the public sector) on training and development in 1991. According to a report published by the University of Twente at the beginning of 1992, total company expenditure (both public and private-sector) on training and development was NFl 8 billion (£2.6 billion). The latest figures from the Central Bureau of Statistics show that the private sector devoted some NFl 3 billion to training in 1990.

There is no compulsory statutory training levy on companies although many sectoral and company agreements detail some kind of training fund, which is set up by agreement between the unions and the employer(s), and financed by mandatory contributions. As far as apprenticeships go, companies are required only to fund the in-house, on-the-job training aspects, with general theoretical education taking place at external institutions, which are funded jointly by government, regional authorities and the companies using them.

An important development over the past few years has been the widespread inclusion of training schemes in collective agreements. Although the scope of such initiatives is limited unions have been willing to limit pay increases in exchange for improved training facilities and opportunities.

In addition, the government has moved towards greater decentralization of education and training over the past few years, retaining control over budgetary expenditure, but ceding more regional and municipal control over the budget allocations. Various elements of current legislation (*Arbeidsvoorzieningswet, Kaderwet Volwasseneneducatie* and *Wet Sectorvorming en Vernieuwing van het Middelbaar Beroepsonderwijs*) are to be combined in 1996. This is to make educational paths more flexible, to increase the opportunities of continuing education for the less qualified, to step up co-operation between education and employment, and to increase the influence of employers on educational content. It is also intended to harmonize certain qualifications, especially for apprentices and MBO students.

Appendix 8.1 Qualifications held by the work force (as a percentage of the total), 1990

Over 6·5 per cent of GNP is spent on education, second only to Sweden in the OECD.

Sex	Basic	MAVO	LBO	HAVO / VWO	MBO	HBO	University
Men	12·3	6·5	19·1	4·7	36·3	12·9	7·7
Women	10·3	11·1	16·6	6·5	34·4	16·3	4·3
Total	11·5	8·2	18·2	5·4	35·6	14·2	6·5

Source: Ministry of Labour.

Appendix 8.2 Organizations

Ministry of Education and Science:
Postbus 25000
Europaweg 4
2700 LZ Zoetermeer
tel. + 31 79 53 19 11
fax + 31 79 51 20 89

Ministry of Social Affairs and
Employment:
Postbus 20801
2600 EV The Hague
tel. + 31 70 333 4444
fax + 31 70 371 4555

Central Employment Service
(Arbeidsvoorziening):
Postbus 437
Visseringlaan 26
2280 AK Rijswijk
tel. + 31 70 313 0911
fax + 31 70 313 0630

Chapter 9

Portugal

The issue of training and development is at the centre of political debate in Portugal. On the country's accession to the European Community the Commission acknowledged the need for the Portuguese economy to modernize and develop along the lines of its European partners and to prepare for the single market. As a result, a five-year Specific Programme for Industrial Development in Portugal (PEDIP) was launched in 1989, providing for regional development within a framework of action in four priority areas. One of the four objectives was to provide 'stronger foundations for basic and further vocational training for careers in industry'. The PEDIP attracts direct EC funding in addition to funds channelled through the European Social Fund.

An interim Commission report on the implementation of the programme, published in 1990, concluded that 'for several decades Portugal has been virtually without an active vocational training policy' apart from selected schemes, set up in the mid-1980s, aimed at young people. It found no systematic assessment of industry's specific training requirements and in consequence there was a shortage of skilled personnel to meet these needs. The purpose of PEDIP is to improve human resources in industry, particularly those of entrepreneurs and executives, senior and middle technical management and technical specialists. One of the guiding principles of PEDIP has been to develop the concept of partnership in training intitiatives.

However, the development issues go far beyond the lack of skilled specialists in industry. Portugal not only has the lowest proportion of qualified personnel in the EC but also the highest rate of illiteracy – possibly as high as 20 per cent of the population – making the raising of general education levels, as well as occupational skill, a national priority. The national education and training systems have both been subjected to radical reform. Many changes are in the process of being implemented, hence, whilst broad principles have been set down, it is too early to assess the impact of the changes.

The role of the European Social Fund

The European Social Fund, which co-finances vocational training and job creation schemes throughout the Community, plays a pivotal role in Portugal. Objective 1 of the fund's programme (there are five in all) is to assist regions whose development is lagging, notably where per capita GDP is 75 per cent or less than the Community average, which applies to all regions of Portugal. Between 1989 and 1993 some Ecu 2,447 million (at 1989 prices) or £3,495 million of Social Fund money will be allocated to Portugal, under Objective 1, for developing human resources. Over half is earmarked for adult training, but significant sums will go to improving the general education system (about 25 per cent) and basic training for young people (some 17 per cent). This represents over a third of all European Community support framework money allocated to underdeveloped regions.

Projects are supported on a co-funded basis, with the Social Fund providing up to 75 per cent of eligible public spending and the balance made up from the national budget, the social security budget and a small percentage from promoting organizations. After agreement between the Commission and the national authorities on priorities and actions, Social Fund finance is channelled through operational programmes into specific training courses. The Department for European Social Fund Affairs (DAFSE, Departamento para os Assuntos do Fundo Social Europeu) is the arm of the Ministry of Employment and Social Security responsible for financing and co-ordinating these activities.

The education system

The 1986 Education Act (*Lei de bases do sistema educativo*, law No. 46/86) brought in a comprehensive reform of the entire education system. Until 1986 compulsory schooling covered just six years, from the ages of 6 to 12, provided in the primary sector, after which young people could enter the labour market. Under the new legislation, which will apply fully to students who started school in the academic year 1987/8, compulsory schooling is extended to nine years, ending at the age of 15 or 16. At this point, students may choose whether to continue secondary education, possibly in preparation for higher education, go into vocational training or seek employment.

The Act also embraces areas such as adult education, distance learning, Portuguese as a second language and vocational education. The broad principles of a new vocational training system are laid down in the Act (and fleshed out by subsequent legislation), including the accrediting of individual training modules leading to recognized qualifications.

Vocational education is provided in the form of initial education for those who have completed compulsory schooling, through the mainstream schools system, new training colleges or arrangements with other bodies. The Act also envisages giving employees greater opportunities to continue their education by improving, updating or converting their skills. Higher general education standards are to be achieved through programmes aimed at combating illiteracy and inequality of opportunity.

Basic education

Basic education (*ensino básico*) is compulsory and divided into three consecutive cycles. The first two cycles (lasting four and two years respectively) are taught in primary school. The first covers basic skills whilst the second, taught between the ages of ten and twelve, encompasses subjects such as Portuguese, a foreign language, mathematics, history, the natural sciences as well as the visual arts, music, crafts and physical education. The third cycle, standard secondary education (*ensino secundário unificado*), lasts three years and comprises general courses continuing most of the subjects of the second cycle, with the introduction of a second foreign language. Students completing this cycle receive a secondary education diploma (*diploma do ensino secundário*).

Thereafter students may continue for a further three years at school:

- On the academic track in preparation for higher education, or
- On the vocational track through a three-year technical course, or they may:
- Undertake initial vocational training at a training college
- Enter an apprenticeship (see next section), or
- Enter the labour market (see next section).

Higher secondary education

Higher secondary education (*ensino secundário complementar*) is composed of two cycles lasting two years and one year respectively. The first cycle gives more specialized courses, divided into option groups, each with an academic as well as a vocational component. The five options broadly cover the natural sciences, science and technology, the social sciences, the humanities and finally the arts, with Portuguese, a foreign language and philosophy compulsory for all option groups. All include a vocational element. The final year of secondary education essentially provides preparatory courses geared to entry into higher education (*diploma de fim de estudos secondários*).

School technical education. Three-year technical education courses established in secondary schools from 1983 to qualify students up to intermediate level (level II – eleventh grade) continue to provide the majority of students with basic vocational training. There are thirty-five such courses (some of them now also run by training colleges) run by state and private secondary schools and attended by over 20,000 students. They include a general and a technical education component as well as a company placement in appropriate cases. On completion, students obtain a technical education diploma (*diploma de formação técnico-profissional*) in a specific discipline, which corresponds to a higher secondary education diploma and allows transfer to higher education, or to a *certificado de qualificação profissional* at level III (the end of full technical schooling).

In the academic year 1991/2 the most popular courses were accountancy (1,733 students enrolled), secretarial studies (4,478), electronics (1,773), electrical installation (1,949), information technology (2,163), information management (2,992), and engineering maintenance (1,332).

This type of training has been criticized as too removed from the needs of industry, the major impetus for the development of the new technical training colleges.

Training colleges (escolas profissionais). Training colleges were established only in 1989 (under decree law 26/89) on a decentralized basis, under the aegis of the Education Ministry, as an alternative to mainstream higher secondary education. They aim to increase vocational training, especially to the level of intermediate technician (*quadros medios*), at the same time as meeting identifiable local and sectoral development needs. Colleges may be founded on the initiative of bodies such as local authorities, the social partners and co-operative societies which together apply for approval from GETAP (Gabinete de Educação Technológica, Artistica e Profissional), the official body responsible for supervising this type of education. The promoters of a project are expected to continue their participation in the running of the college after its establishment.

By 1992 some 140 local technical colleges had been established, attracting over 11,000 students. (This compares with over 25,000 students undertaking technical training elsewhere – including within secondary education, though some courses are run at both types of institution.) Courses are designed for those who have completed the nine years of compulsory education, or those with six years' education and additional equivalent training. The colleges run three-year courses (equivalent to the tenth, eleventh and twelfth years of higher secondary education), with 50 per cent of teaching hours (totalling 1,200 annually) allocated to technical and practical subjects and 25 per cent each to general education and science. At the end of a course students are awarded a *certificado de qualificação profissional* at level III, which corresponds to the completion of full secondary schooling, enabling them to transfer to higher education or enter the labour market.

A level I qualification is equivalent to tenth-year schooling, i.e. one year on top of the nine years' compulsory schooling. Level II is equivalent to the eleventh year, level III to the completion of full secondary schooling, level IV to complete secondary schooling plus some technical education and level V to complete tertiary education.

In the 1991/2 academic year the most popular options included basic computing (for which 1,545 students enrolled), accountancy (700), civil engineering (427), hotel reception, catering and management (455) and tourism (329).

Higher education

The 1986 education reform also affected higher education, and changes were implemented from the beginning of the 1989/90 academic year. These will be evaluated after three years.

Tertiary education takes place at both public and private universities and polytechnics. Whilst the Ministry of Education has a supervisory role regarding the private sector, it has overall responsibility for the public sector, although individual institutions are self-governing and award their own degrees. Both types of institution offer a wide range of courses, though polytechnics tend to be more orientated towards the professions.

In order to enter higher education, various conditions must be met. Firstly, students who have completed twelve years of education, or the equivalent, must take the national general entrance examination (*prova geral de acesso*, PGA). This assesses intellectual and cultural development and the use of the Portuguese language. (In 1992 there were widespread student protests against the cultural bias of the examination, which, opponents claim, favours those from advantaged backgrounds.) Secondly, individual institutions set their own conditions of entry to each course. They normally specify that certain subjects must be studied in the tenth to twelfth years of secondary education. In addition, institutions may set their own examinations.

Every year the Ministry of Education publishes a comprehensive list of entry requirements for all courses on which the number of places available is limited. Thus entry to a course will depend on results from secondary education subjects, the PGA exam and any specific examination requirement. Every establishment gives a weighting to each of the three criteria, within specified limits. A central government office is subsequently responsible for placing students on courses, taking students' preferences into account also.

Special competitions for access to higher education are held for candidates who do not meet the general entry requirements, including those:

- Over 25 without the standard entrance qualifications but who have passed a special exam assessing their suitability.
- Already holding a medium or higher-level course qualification.
- From other higher education systems (i.e. outside the scope of the Ministry of Education or abroad).

Universities. University education is provided through thirteen public universities, an Open University and two university institutes not yet designated as universities. Three main degrees are conferred:

- *Licenciado* (full degree after four or six years' study, with graduates typically aged 22 or 24).
- *Mestre* (master's degree after an additional one or two years' academic study, after which a dissertation must be submitted).
- *Doutor* (doctorate degree following three to six years' research).

Subjects offered are education, the fine arts, the arts and humanities, the social sciences, management, law, science, mathematics, engineering and technology, architecture, communications, medicine and agriculture.

Non-university higher education. Polytechnic education (*ensino politécnico*) became established after 1979, and particularly after 1986. There are over fifty establishments within this network, including eight higher schools of management and technology. There is an emphasis on the professions, and the fields of study include marketing, accountancy, administration, public relations, etc. The degrees offered are the *bacharel* (bachelor's first degree after three years' study, graduates aged 21 or 22) or the DESE (*diploma de estudos superiores especializados*), broadly equivalent to a full degree or *licenciado* awarded by a university and taken by those already holding a *bacharel* or *licenciado* degree.

Certificates and diplomas may be awarded for shorter courses in both the university and the polytechnic sectors.

There are in addition some higher institutes under joint ministerial control, as well as private higher education institutions, which are regulated by statute, four of them recognized as universities. (There is also a Portuguese Catholic university established by Rome.) These latter are assuming greater importance as the growing demand for higher education can no longer be met by state establishments.

Liaison between universities and polytechnics. The two systems are closely linked and students can transfer between universities and polytechnics, as indeed they can between public and private institutions.

Enrolment in higher education. Enrolment in higher education has risen rapidly in recent years. The number of students enrolled in state higher education rose from 107,977 in the academic year 1988/9 to 132,441 in the academic year 1990/1. The respective figures for enrolment in private institutions increased from 28,468 to 49,797 over the same period.

Science education (including maths, computer science and engineering) is comparatively well developed. In 1988 some 24 per cent of students took a science degree, compared with 16 per cent in Italy, 24 per cent in Sweden and 30 per cent in Germany.

Vocational training

Objectives of vocational training

The principal aims of Portugal's vocational training system were stated in the tripartite agreement (*acordo de politica de formação profissional*) signed by the government, the two main trade union confederations, the CGTP-IN and the UGT, as well as by the employers grouped in the three principal confederations, the CCP, CIP and CAP, in July 1991. This accord forms part of the overall Economic and Social Agreement (*acordo económico e social*, AES) aimed at developing the economy as a whole.

Four broad objectives were defined:

- To promote training in order to meet the country's needs adequately.
- To raise the level of educational qualifications.
- To enhance the efficiency of existing structures.
- To strengthen the role of the social partners.

The agreement acknowledges the need for a better link between training and employment, and an intensified focus upon continuing education.

Framework legislation

This agreement was subsequently incorporated into various pieces of legislation. The first law on the subject, decree law 401/91, promulgated on 16 October 1991, created a framework for initial and continuing vocational training.

The legislation outlines the broad role of the various partners in the training field. The state is largely responsible for launching programmes targeted at initial training and at specific groups on the labour market, promoting the training of trainers and anticipating training needs, whilst companies are expected to focus on continuing training, including on-the-job training, adaptation to new technology, and improving product and productivity.

The aim is to set up a comprehensive and flexible training system, using methods such as block release courses, *stages*, employment training, work experience and modular courses. Training may be delivered through mainstream education, through publicly or jointly run training centres and other training organizations, as well as in co-operation with companies, professional associations (or employers or unions), local authorities and cultural associations.

Training activity is to be subject to official certification, which will outline the necessary vocational or corresponding academic qualifications required for different jobs or groups of jobs. Certification will take into account the nature of the course and the experience of the worker.

State involvement in training

The responsibilities of individual agencies under the framework legislation are fleshed out in decree law 405/91.

The Ministry of Employment supervises and co-ordinates training policy between various Ministries. Its Directorate of Employment and Vocational Training formulates policy, whilst a separate Institute of Employment and Vocational Training (Instituto do Emprego do Formação Profissional, IEFP) executes it. European Social Fund projects are generally administered by the IEFP, which must get funding approval from DAFSE (see above).

The IEFP (set up in 1986) has overall responsibility for promoting vocational information and guidance, and for the training, retraining and placement of workers, particularly young people and those at a disadvantage in the labour market. Representatives of government and the social partners sit on its managing board and supervisory committee.

The IEFP conducts research to identify training needs, which is used to develop and evaluate training activities carried out by regional vocational training centres and other IEFP-sponsored organizations. One central department deals with training trainers, and another with management development. Some 2,500 of its 3,500 staff work in the country's five regions, each with a tripartite advisory committee, which run seventy employment centres, twenty vocational training centres and two employment and vocational training centres.

A new Employment Monitoring Unit has been set up, under the aegis of the IEFP. It will be responsible for monitoring developments and collecting information on employment and vocational training at national and regional levels in order to assess training needs.

State vocational training centres (centros de formação profissional de gestão directa/protocolares)
Some twenty schools located in the regions provide training of a

technical and practical nature lasting between six and twelve months leading to an initial qualification or conversion of skills. The courses are intended for students aged 18 or over who have not completed (nine years') compulsory education but who can read and write. More specialized courses are available for students with ninth- to eleventh-grade schooling. Trainees receive an allowance related to the statutory national minimum wage. Around 15,500 received such training on the mainland in 1991.

Co-managed vocational training centres (centros de formação profissional de gestão participada)
Public resources are available through the IEFP for permanent training supporting the activities of one or more industrial sectors. Currently twenty-seven such centres exist, for the food, textile and construction industries, among others. In 1991 some 40,000 employees benefited from schemes run by these centres.

Training through agreement (formação em cooperação – acordos)
Since 1985 funds have been available to support one-off training activities run through agreements with employers and private, public and co-operative training providers. Grants are available for up to 75 per cent of running costs and loans up to half the cost of equipment or building works.

Apprenticeships

Aprendizagem: formação profissional de jovens em regime de alternância (decree law 102/84, revised by 436/88)
The existing apprenticeship system was launched in 1984 and reformed in 1988. The National Apprenticeship Commission (CNA), an arm of the IEFP, together with its regional committees, co-ordinates and subsidizes apprenticeship programmes (and the new apprenticeship induction course, see below). These last from one to four years, depending on the number of years' secondary education students have completed, and are organized as sandwich courses. There is a general education component (Portuguese, maths, current affairs) which, together with technical training, is undertaken at a recognized training centre; practical training is with a company. Apprenticeships are geared towards those aged 14–24 who have completed compulsory education and are looking for their first job.

Apprentices are bound to the employer under contract but are paid a grant, set by the Ministry of Employment annually, to which companies have to contribute 100 per cent in the first year, tapering down to 35 per cent in the fourth year. They also receive assistance with travel and subsistence expenses. (Apprenticeship is one of the operational programmes which enjoys support from EC funds.) On completion of an apprenticeship, trainees are awarded a *certificado de aptidão profissional* (CAP), which is equivalent to the appropriate number of years' schooling. Over 15,500 young people participated in such schemes in 1991. (According to the EC comparability criteria, the CAP is deemed to be equivalent to a UK NVQ level III in the metalworking trade.)

Apprenticeship induction course. In 1991 an apprenticeship induction course of between one and two years was introduced for trainees between the ages of 15 and 21 who have not completed six years' compulsory education. These combine general education and practical skills to equip young people to enter an apprenticeship or even to re-enter mainstream education. On completing a course, the trainee will receive a certificate equivalent to having completed the second cycle of basic education (see above) and a vocational qualification equivalent to level I, conferred jointly by the Ministries of Education and Employment.

A variety of organizations can run such courses, including education or training centres, companies and professional associations. The course must be established by a written contract detailing:

- The parties to the contract.
- The objective of the course.
- The location/s where the training will be undertaken.
- Its length, which may not exceed 150 hours in total, seven hours daily or thirty-five weekly.

Of the total hours, sixteen must be divided equally between general educational subjects (Portuguese, maths, English or French and current affairs) and no more than nineteen may be vocational. Time spent at a work station must not exceed 20 per cent of the total allocation.

Trainees will be entitled to various allowances (food, lodging) as well as 40 per cent of the amount set by the Ministry of Education for apprenticeships (see above).

Programmes receiving EC funding

As mentioned earlier, there are a number of broad programmes through which EC and public funds are channelled to support training activities. Each programme defines the type of measures to be supported, the objective of that particular type of training and the level of qualification to be achieved, the target group, and the average length of course. Most of the training is administered by the IEFP and funded by Social Fund and public money.

PEDIP. The major exception is vocational training under the PEDIP programme. Such training activity is specifically aimed at strengthening the technological infrastructure of industry, and is targeted at graduates already working or wishing to work in industry, and at senior and middle-ranking technicians (i.e. those who have completed full secondary education). The scope of activities which can be funded is extensive and falls under nine headings, including new technology, management courses, research and training functions. Public subsidies are available for up to 90 per cent of training projects.

European Social Fund programmes. As far as the IEFP operational programmes are concerned, these fall under the following heads:

- Training of those in employment – ranging from initial training programmes to action to improve training levels and reconverting skills – including managers and technicians.
- Improvement of training structures and promoting jobs.
- Vocational training for young people through sandwich courses.
- Advanced training in information technology.
- Training for long-term unemployed adults.

Training for the disabled. Technical and financial support is available for office amenities, for equipment and for hiring monitors for programmes aimed at young people aged 12 and above. State vocational rehabilitation centres were set up from 1985 with the aim of providing disabled people aged 17 with the skills to hold down a job, or the opportunity to gain a vocational qualification. The training is vocational in agriculture, industry and services with sheltered employment.

Training for women (formação e emprego de mulheres). The programme was set up in 1980 and is now receiving support from the

European Social Fund to help unemployed women gain work in new employment, management or traditionally male-dominated jobs. Such courses are run either by the IEFP or by other accredited bodies (including companies, employers' associations or trades unions). They last between 120 and 280 hours, and 1,426 women attended such courses in 1991. A training survey showed that women were four times less likely to be involved in training than men.

Preparing young people for the world of work. This programme (*inserção de jovens na vida profissional*, IJOVIP) is aimed at those between 18 and 25 who have completed secondary education, are registered at an employment centre and are seeking their first job. It lasts nine months and provides practical technical training as well as work experience. Trainees receive an allowance, equivalent to the national minimum wage, which is at least 75 per cent subsidized by the IEFP (100 per cent in the case of disabled people or women seeking to enter male-dominated jobs). In 1991 some 12,800 trainees participated in the scheme. Companies must meet certain criteria in order to qualify for it. If a permanent job is offered to a trainee, then the company receives a lump-sum payment of twelve times the national minimum wage.

Other initiatives. There are also programmes covering particular regions. For example, the programme covering the Setúbal peninsula – a relatively new industrial region – includes training measures targeted at particular sectors, such as manufacturing, business and services, tourism, small enterprises, the environment.

Individuals in employment or without a job may apply to their local employment centre for a grant (provided by the IEFP) to undertake training on their own initiative. Priority is given to employees in sectors or companies undergoing restructuring or in difficulties, or to those with a low level of training. Companies must give their authorisation for this arrangement. Basic pay is maintained during the training period.

Management education and training

Management training and induction
(*formação e integração de quadros*, FIQ)

This initiative aims to improve job prospects for better qualified students, that is, those who have either followed technical training courses in their final years at secondary school or undertaken further training elsewhere. Programmes last between nine months and a year, depending on course level, and include a theoretical component and a company placement. Trainees receive a grant, payable by the company of Esc 52,200 monthly (£243) for middle-level courses, and Esc 80,200 monthly (£374) for higher courses. The grant is paid entirely by the state where such training opens up access for women to traditionally male jobs, or for disabled trainees. If a permanent contract is offered at the end of the training, as frequently happens (see below), the company receives a lump sum equal to twelve times the national minimum wage. Some 1,417 young people on the mainland took part in this programme in 1991.

Executive training

There is a distinct difference in executives' level of qualification, depending upon age group. Those under 35 tend to have graduated with a *licenciado* degree, whereas the majority of those over 40 completed full secondary schooling but are not graduates. Because market conditions have changed so rapidly in the last decade, companies usually prefer to recruit younger, better qualified people into management positions, even though they have less business experience. The preferred degree subjects are economics and management, rather than law or engineering, which were more popular a decade ago. Degrees from the Instituto Superior de Gestão, the Instituto Superior de Ciências do Trabalho e da Empresa and the Catholic University (UCP) are highly valued. MBAs are rare, although some higher education institutions now run courses. Companies are fast increasing their investment in management training. A recent study showed that the average manager was engaged on ten to fifteen days' training a year.

The current situation

Substantial public funds are being directed towards a variety of training activities, mostly with the aid of the European Social Fund. Therefore newly established businesses with training needs (either for existing or for potential staff) would need to approach the local technical colleges or training centres to see whether they were already running specific courses or might do so in the future. Inter-enterprise training centres are planned shortly, offering a wide range of subject areas, to promote regular vocational training in small and medium-sized enterprises located in the same area. As regards in-company training, applications for funding need to be made initially through the local employment centres, which then direct them through regional to national organizations. Funding normally covers most of trainee grants and wages for employees on training.

There is as yet no statutory right to time off for training but legislation is in the pipeline.

The impact of vocational training

In 1991, with the assistance of EC funds, the Ministry of Employment carried out a survey of 3,776 manufacturing companies employing ten or more staff to assess the impact of vocational training over the period 1986–90. Detailed data were obtained from an indicative sample of firms.

In 1986 a mere 5·7 per cent of firms surveyed were involved in vocational training programmes. The figure rose to 13·5 per cent in 1989 but dropped back again to 11·1 per cent in 1990. The extent of involvement increased with size of firm; whilst only 6·4 per cent of small firms (under fifty staff) participated in training in 1990, 16·4 per cent of medium-sized firms (up to 100), 30·6 per cent of large firms (up to 499) and 61·1 per cent of the largest firms (with more than 500 staff and mostly in the public sector) did so. By sector, the greatest participation was in metalworking (where 27 per cent of all firms had been involved in training), chemicals and petroleum (25 per cent), metal products and transport, and textiles (both 17 per cent). Of the total trainees involved, 81 per cent were company employees and 12 per cent unemployed persons seeking their first job. Some 48 per cent of the latter were subsequently taken on by the firms which had trained them; there are a variety of financial incentives for this.

Although public subsidy – largely from the European Social Fund – still accounts for most funding, its share fell from 78 per cent of the total in 1986 to 65 per cent in 1990, with private funds increasing from 20 per cent to 28 per cent over the period.

Benefits for firms involved in the training included increased productivity (mentioned by 76 per cent of companies), improved product quality (64 per cent), higher productivity per worker (59 per cent), better working relationships (51 per cent), increased production (50 per cent), more internal staff mobility (44 per cent) and lower staff turnover (40 per cent).

Forecast of training needs

A survey was conducted by the Ministry of Employment in 1990 to evaluate vocational training activity in progress in companies (1,500 outside agriculture) during 1989, and to identify training needs for 1990–2. The results of the 1989 evaluation confirmed that far fewer women than men benefited from training (by a factor of one to four). The average length of training lasted 166 hours and cost Esc 218,300 (Esc 1,300, or £6, per hour).

An average of 40 per cent of all companies surveyed forecast some training needs, 60 per cent in manufacturing, 13 per cent in commerce, hotels and restaurants, 13 per cent in services, 9 per cent in construction. Companies estimated that most of their needs could be met by in-company training, with support from state vocational training centres and training colleges. Some 57 per cent of training needs identified involved improving the skills of those who already held a qualification, and in 26 per cent of cases they were for a first qualification. The volume of training needs was greatest for production workers, administrators and scientists and technicians, with subjects involving new technology, materials technology and automation. The areas of skill shortage identified were mainly job-related, especially in the use of computers, civil engineering, marketing, and languages.

Appendix 9.1 Distribution of the work force by qualification (as a percentage of the total), 1981–91

Level of qualification	1981	1991
Senior white-collar	1·5	2·2
Middle-ranking white-collar	1·6	2·0
Supervisors/first-line managers	3·8	4·1
Qualified staff (full secondary education, at least)	42·5	43·2
Semi-qualified (first-stage secondary schooling)	20·8	18·1
Unqualified	12·2	10·8
Trainees and apprentices	8·9	11·6
Not known	9·7	8·0

Source: DEMESS.

Appendix 9.2 Organizations

Ministry of Labour and Social
Security (Ministério do Emprego e
da Segurança Social, MESS):
Praça de Londres 2
1100 Lisboa
tel. + 351 1 80 44 60

Institute of Employment and
Vocational Training (Instituto do
Emprego do Formação Profissional,
IEFP):
Avenida José Malhoa 11
1100 Lisboa
tel. + 351 1 726 25 36

Department of European Social Fund
Affairs (Departamento para os
Assuntos do Fundo Social Europeu,
DAFSE):
Avenida Almirante Reis 72
1100 Lisboa
tel. + 351 1 814 14 50

Office of Technological, Artistic and
Vocational Education (Gabinete de
Educação Tecnológica Artistica e
Profissional,
GETAP: a section of the Ministry of
Education):
Avenida 24 Julho 140
1300 Lisboa
tel. + 351 1 395 34 07

Association of Portuguese Human
Resource Managers (Associação
Portuguesa dos Gestores e Técnicos
dos Recursos Humanos, APG):
Avenida do Brasil 194
1700 Lisboa
tel. + 351 1 89 97 66
fax + 351 1 80 93 40

Office in Oporto:
Rua Formosa 49
4000 Oporto
tel. + 351 2 32 32 34
fax + 351 2 200 07 64

Confederation of Portuguese
Industry (Confederação da Indústria
Portuguesa, CIP: the central
employers' organization for
industry):
Avenida 5 de Outubro 35
1000 Lisboa
tel. + 351 1 54 74 54

Confederation of Portuguese
Commerce (Confederação do
Comércio Portugues, CCP: the
central employers' organization in
trade and commerce):
Rua Saraiva de Carvalho 1
1000 Lisboa

Confederação Geral dos
Trabalhadores
Portugueses–Intersindical Nacional
(CGTP–IN):
Rua Vitor Cordon 1
1200 Lisboa
tel. + 351 1 34 72 181/8

União Geral de Trabalhadores
(UGT)
Rua Buenos Aires 11
1200 Lisboa
tel. + 351 1 67 65 03/5

British–Portuguese Chamber of
Commerce
Rua da Estrela 8
1200 Lisboa
tel. + 351 1 67 65 03/5

Chapter 10
Spain

Initial and intermediate vocational training takes place through a vocational option within the education system. Traditionally seen as a path for the academically less gifted, and criticized by employers for lack of direct relevance, vocational training is being overhauled to raise and refine skill levels. Proposals are expected for major changes, especially at intermediate level, during the course of the 1990s.

The low level of interest in training among many indigenous companies has generated trade union efforts to secure training provision through collective agreement, with a variety of agreed arrangements on time off, funding, joint regulation of training, and a commitment to employee development. Shortages of suitably qualified managers, reflected in rapidly rising managerial pay, have given a boost to business education and led to a proliferation of private training providers.

Secondary and tertiary education

The secondary and tertiary education system is in the throes of substantial reform. Under the law reforming education (the LOGSE), passed in November 1991, considerable changes will be introduced during the next five years which will affect all levels of education. At the time of writing (1992) the old system largely prevails, but the changes are being introduced from the lower levels upwards. These will also affect vocational training and higher education in the next few years. The reforms profoundly affect both the structure and the curriculum of primary and secondary schooling.

Secondary education

Entrants to the secondary school system will now have compulsory education from 6 to 16 (prior to the LOGSE it was 6 to 14), known as *Educación general básica* (EGB). From 14 to 17 there is an 'academic' secondary level (broadly similar to the English A level), which leads on to the BUP certificate (*bachillerato unificado y polivalente*). Those students wishing to prepare for university entry then take a one-year course known as a *curso de orientación universitaria* (COU), and sit competitive entrance examinations for the university to which they apply, known as *selectividad*. Students graduating from the basic general education (EGB) require a *título de escolaridad* (roughly equivalent to the UK GCSE) to progress to on to the *bachillerato* course.

School students who fail to gain the *título de escolaridad* but obtain a school leaving certificate (*certificado de escolaridad*) may proceed to the parallel full-time vocational training programme (*formación profesional*). This consists of two years' first-stage vocational training (roughly equivalent to the UK BTEC) and a second stage of three years (*formación profesional superior*) which is roughly equivalent to HND. This represents one of the prime forms in which initial and intermediate training is delivered.

At present approximately 1·65 million pupils are pursuing the *bachillerato*, with 870,000 in initial vocational training (*formación profesional*).

The system requires a student to achieve target levels of competence in order to pass on to the next year's study. Some 25 per cent of pupils have to repeat a year for this reason, and therefore finish their studies later than anticipated. This problem is most acute in the first stage of vocational training, where in 1990/1 53 per cent of students failed to pass on to the second stage, and 30 per cent of second-stage students failed. It is also a serious problem at EGB level, where in 1990/1 22 per cent of eighth-grade students had to resit. Twenty-two per cent of *bachillerato* and university preparatory course students were also unsuccessful.

Education remains largely under the control of the Ministry of Education and Science, but powers are gradually being devolved to the autonomous communities. To date Catalonia, Andalucia, the Basque country, Galicia, Valencia, the Canary Islands, Navarre and La Rioja have these powers, while the other nine autonomous communities still depend on central government.

The educational reforms include extending the EGB to 16 and merging the upper year of the *bachillerato* and the university preparatory course (COU). In September 1992 the reforms began with the first two years' intake (aged 6 and 7); these students are now described as following *educación primaria* instead of *educación general basica* – a term which is to be phased out. As yet, even these reforms are being adopted unevenly across the autonomous communities, not all of which are geared up to implement them.

Higher education

There are forty universities, four of which are controlled by the Catholic church: all are regulated by the Higher Education Reform Act, 1983. There are different types of higher education institution, each of which teaches to different levels of degree (see below). Students enter university by completing either the higher school preparatory course (COU) or the second-stage vocational training course (*formación profesional superior*), followed by *selectividad*. Applicants are admitted if their performance in *selectividad* together with their COU grades reaches a prescribed level. In 1992 some 330,000 students sat COU and it is estimated that 175,000 will attempt *selectividad*. Normally around 85 per cent of *selectividad* candidates are successful.

University courses are structured in three 'cycles'. The first, of three years, leads to a diploma qualification, the second, of two years' more specialized study, leads to a master's degree (*licenciatura*), and the third, of two more years, to a doctorate.

Students enrol in a *facultad*, an *escuela técnica superior*, an *escuela universitaria*, an *escuela técnica universitaria* or a *colegio universitario*. These offer courses of differing length and level. In the *facultad*, students follow a five or six-year course leading to a *licenciatura* (roughly equivalent to an MA). In the *escuela superior universitaria* students of technical subjects such as engineering or architecture follow a six-year course leading to the qualification of *ingeniero superior*. In the *escuela universitaria* a three-year course leads to a *diploma*, in the *escuela técnica universitaria* a three-year course leads to a *diploma* in technical subjects, and in the *colegio universitario* a student follows the first three years of a *licenciatura* before transferring to complete the more advanced stages at a *facultad*. The *colegio universitario* will often be in a provincial centre (such as Gerona) and the *facultad* will be in the regional capital (such as Barcelona).

In 1986 30 per cent of Spaniards aged 18–24 entered higher education (up from 20 per cent in 1975). Figures for 1990/1 show 1,099,313 students in higher education – an age participation rate similar to that of advanced EC countries. The students are substantially concentrated in Madrid, Barcelona and Andalucia, which between them account for

50 per cent of total university places. Students normally study at their local university, unless the course they wish to follow is not available.

The distribution of higher education students across the academic disciplines has given rise to considerable concern. A study by the Ministry of Education and Science in January 1992 suggested that Spanish students are considerably out of line with most other EC countries in this respect. There are a greater proportion of students reading law and social sciences than in any other EC country (about 30 per cent); the proportion of humanities students, at 17 per cent, is close to the EC average, but there are fewer students of technical subjects than in any other EC country (engineering and the natural sciences combined account for 25 per cent). According to OECD figures only 14 per cent of Spanish students graduate in a science or engineering discipline, compared with 30–35 per cent in France and Germany. Graduate unemployment tends to be concentrated in the social sciences and humanities. For example, whilst 99 per cent of IT, maths, physics, engineering and business studies graduates found immediate employment (if not necessarily in a relevant field), the percentage for geography and history was 76 per cent each, and in languages it was 84 per cent.

There is also a disproportionately large percentage of students following lengthy degree courses: some 70 per cent are on courses lasting six years. Drop-out rates are also high by international standards, especially at bachelor degree level, where just over half of all students fail to complete their course, according to OECD figures.

Vocational training

Vocational education and training take place within the school system (see above) and through a wide variety of schemes for both the employed and the unemployed. The overall framework is set by the government's National Training and Development Plan (*Plan Nacional de Formación e Inserción Profesional*), issued orginally in 1985, and most recently updated in 1990 (royal decree 1618/1990). The plan is presided over by the Vocational Training Council (Consejo General de Formación Profesional), established in 1986. The council is a tripartite body, with thirteen representatives each of the trade unions, the employers and government.

Its task is to oversee the organization of initial training schemes for the unemployed and refresher courses for existing employees through the agency of the National Employment Institute (Instituto Nacional de Empleo, INEM). The figures suggest that in early 1992 there were some 312,000 trainees following courses under this plan, of whom 67 per cent were unemployed, and 57 per cent aged over 25. On average their courses lasted 600 hours. Twenty per cent of the courses take place in INEM establishments, the remainder in 'collaborating centres' (trade union establishments, employers' organizations, companies and private-sector training establishments).

Until April 1992 trainees often received grants for attending courses; 200,000 were receiving 75 per cent of the legal monthly minimum wage, or Pta 40,000 (£235). However, these grants were abolished as part of the government's 'Convergence Plan', designed to trim public spending in the approach to European monetary union.

The most popular courses were in management studies, IT, business administration, construction and tourism. Least numerous were courses in agriculture and fisheries, mining, conservation and mineral processing.

Of the total of 21,500 courses offered, 12,300 were at starter level, 5,400 were for a recognized qualification, 3,350 for a specialist qualification and 472 for retraining. The make-up of the total of about 300,000 trainees involved was as follows. Just over 50 per cent (161,000) were young long-term unemployed; 104,000 were in employment, self-employed or members of co-operatives, and 33,000 were farmworkers or retrainees. Some 5,000 training instructors received training. The overall pass rate was 94 per cent. Of the 286,000 successful trainees, 145,000 were female and 141,000 male.

Training schemes

The National Training Plan categorizes training schemes into the following main categories:

- Vocational training for young people and the long-term unemployed.
- Sandwich courses for those under 25 and full-time vocational training students.
- Retraining schemes for those without general basic education or first-stage vocational training, sandwich courses for second-stage vocational training students, work experience programmes and university and training schemes for military service graduates.

- Training schemes for sectors or companies undergoing restructuring, and for existing employees.
- Training schemes for women returners and new entrants to the job market.
- Training schemes for students (including co-operation with other EC countries).
- Training schemes for the disabled, migrants and workers' co-operatives.

Under the plan, the national employment service INEM provides assistance and sponsorship for a number of training programmes. Some of the principal individual schemes are outlined below.

Young people aged 16–20 may be employed on special fixed-term training contracts (*contrato para la formación*), lasting from a minimum of three months up to three years, with at least 25–50 per cent of working time spent on training. These can culminate in a vocational training certificate (*título de formación profesional ocupacional*). They may also be entitled to retraining if they have not completed basic primary education. Courses are sponsored by the Ministry of Education and Science and may be run by INEM, by the employer or by a collaborating centre. If the course is in-company, INEM may subsidize it. If the employee is contracted full-time for at least six months, INEM pays the employer Pta 90 per employee/hour (£0·52). Young people who have completed a training contract, are unemployed and received a non-INEM-approved training course during their employment are entitled to a 200 hour training course run by INEM. If the company training is craft-based the employer may receive a subsidy of 75 per cent of the statutory minimum wage for periods ranging from six months to three years. Company training plans require the signed consent of the workers' representatives. INEM issues quarterly reports to provincial steering committees composed of employers and trade union representatives on the scope and nature of the training schemes being operated.

Employers may also apply for subsidies of up to Pta 500 (£2·95) a day for employees on training contracts to attend sandwich courses (funds are provided via European Social Fund projects).

After the training contract provision had been introduced in 1982 the numbers employed on it rose consistently throughout the 1980s – from 20,500 in 1982 to a peak of 331,500 in 1989. Since then the number has fallen back to 260,000 (1991), partly reflecting the shrinking numbers of young people.

A second type of contract used to provide vocational training for new recruits is the work experience contract (*contrato en prácticas*), also introduced in 1982. After peaking at 222,400 trainees in 1989, the 1992 level fell back slightly to 184,000. The contract is aimed at allowing employers to take on graduates, those finishing *formación profesional*, or other qualified school or college leavers, and must begin within four years following completion of their education. As with training contracts, the permitted duration ranges from three months to three years.

The unemployed have access to various schemes. For example, those aged under 25 in vocations identified as suffering shortages of skilled personnel can receive training under an INEM scheme. These are particularly concentrated in new technologies. There are also schemes for those aged 25–30 who have not previously been employed for more than three months, and for the long-term unemployed. Employees whose company is undergoing industrial restructuring can also receive training.

A number of schemes are specifically aimed at women. For example, there are opportunities for women to train in occupations in which they are underrepresented, for women aged over 25 who have been out of paid employment for five years and wish to return to work, and for women with dependants seeking to enter the labour market. These courses are run in conjunction with the Institute for Women (Instituto de la Mujer), and consist of two basic types. In the case of companies prepared to make a firm commitment to taking on female employees the courses can be tailored to the needs of the company; in other cases the training needs of the applicants determine the nature of the course. These courses are offered in the provinces of Madrid, Barcelona, Cáceres, La Coruña, Murcia, Seville, Valencia, Valladolid, Vizcaya and Zaragoza.

Up to April 1992 trainees in many of these categories also received grants equivalent to 75 per cent of the statutory minimum wage during their training. The Convergence Plan abolished the grants and, instead, increased incentives to employers to convert temporary contracts into permanent full-time contracts – for example, initiating a new cash grant of Pta 400,000 (£2,350) to employers who give the under-25s a permanent contract, Pta 500,000 (£2,940) for the over-45s, or women in underrepresented occupations, and Pta 550,000 (£3,235) for those on training or work experience contracts.

Trainees are still, however, eligible for grants when they have to travel to courses, increased for those who need to board. There may also be help towards travel and lodging costs if trainees are obliged to move to another EC state for their training.

Trainers and training establishments

INEM sponsors training courses for trainers (aimed at training 3,000 trainers per year), lasting from 100 to 400 hours for trainers with at least three years' professional experience. In 1991 the government issued regulations to control the administration of the training centres which are officially approved INEM 'collaborating centres'. The regulations include the rates at which it will finance training programmes run in collaborating centres on behalf of INEM. The trainers are to be paid at rates varying from Pta 136 (81p) to Pta 523 per trainee per hour (£3·10), depending on the grade of difficulty of the course, and assuming groups of up to fifteen trainees. INEM also subsidizes the cost of training materials and is prepared to contribute up to 80 per cent of the cost of buildings.

A company wishing to constitute itself as a 'collaborating centre' must meet a number of requirements detailed in a ministerial order issued on 1 April 1991. The requirements include meeting minimum size criteria, providing sufficient equipment and conforming to INEM standards of training content. Employees recruited on training contracts (see above) must be registered at the INEM office, together with a personal training plan (countersigned by the employee representatives and deposited in the local INEM office, where it is available for consultation).

INEM subsidizes the wage costs of trainers who are in employment by compensating the company at a rate of 50 per cent of the statutory minimum wage for the time spent training (subject to funds being available from the European Social Fund).

Regional variations

Some of the autonomous communities also have local training initiatives. An outstanding example is the Basque provinces, where the Basque employers' confederation CONFEBASK has taken new approaches to training. Responding to skill shortages in young job applicants, which have been acute since the closure of traditional apprenticeship training schools (*escuelas de maestria*), the employers started a pioneer programme of 'joint vocational training' in 1991. In sixteen agreements signed with the Basque government, 100 companies have provided practical training for 334 second-stage *formación profesional* students during one-third of their college day. Unlike conventional *formación profesional* courses, these schemes introduce the student to in-company training from the beginning and are designed specifically to train for known company skill shortages. Their success led to the number of participants rising to 600 in 1992. Companies provide training by releasing a production worker to provide instruction. The Basque government dedicates half the budget of its Department of Labour to supporting job creation and training schemes.

Training in large firms

The Economics Ministry conducts an annual survey of collective agreements in Spain's largest companies, covering 1 million employees. This suggests that the provision of company training varies considerably from sector to sector, by size and ownership. In the latest survey 52 per cent of companies with under 500 employees, and 75 per cent of those with over 500 employees, had training programmes. Whereas 54 per cent of Spanish-owned companies provided training, the proportion rose to 80 per cent for foreign-owned private sector companies.

The survey also indicated the features of training programmes: while 28 per cent of existing employees received training, only 4 per cent of new recruits were undergoing training. The average time spent on training was fifty-nine hours per employee per year (3 per cent of agreed working time). There were great differences in this figure according to sector, ranging from nineteen hours in hotels and catering to forty-five hours in financial institutions, sixty-eight hours in metals and electronics and eighty-two hours in non-financial services. Average training costs totalled 1·01 per cent of the total wage bill, with an average Pta 71,000 (£417) spent per trainee in the private sector.

A survey by the trade union UGT of training provision built into collective agreements looked at collective agreements concluded in the first half of 1992. It considered 258 agreements (40 per cent of those in the study, covering 2,002,543 employees) which contained some provision for training. Of these, 151 granted paid leave, 148 gave financial help for study, 120 outlined company training plans, sixty had joint training committees and forty-four provided for joint management of training plans.

Craft training

In 1988 the Ministry of Labour instituted a training programme designed to revive and promote traditional artisan skills which were in danger of neglect. Since then some 60,000 young people have been trained in craft training institutions (*escuelas taller* and *casas de oficio*). Most are situated in historic buildings such as monasteries, castles and stately homes, which themselves are restored under the training programmes and which act as centres for the revival and promotion of local crafts and materials. The programme is considered one of the most successful features of Spain's vocational training, and is being adopted in several Latin American countries.

Future developments

In autumn 1992, government proposals for a substantial reform of the vocational training system were still awaited. The current structure, with its school-based system of *formación profesional*, has been criticized by the employers' confederations as both insufficiently geared to the needs of the labour market and overgeneralized. Reform proposals, probably to be phased in over a seven-year period, are expected to address these issues by introducing a new three-year higher-level *formación profesional* qualification, for which entrants would have to meet university-level admission requirements (the *bachillerato* and one-year preparatory course). The new proposals are also expected to make training programmes more local in nature, tailored to specific local labour market demands; to promote 'joint training programmes', similar to the Basque initiatives mentioned above; and to establish specialized centres for particular trades and professions, and continuing training for trainers.

Management education and training

Private-sector business schools

Spanish executive pay rose strongly throughout the 1980s, to match, and in some cases exceed in real terms, the highest levels in Europe by the early 1990s. One of the main reasons was a shortage of qualified managers during a period of rapid growth and structural change. It has been estimated that there was an unmet demand for some 10,000 MBAs annually during the boom of the late 1980s. To a considerable extent this reflects the failure of the state-run university system to develop sufficient postgraduate business programmes, although state-run business schools (*escuelas de negocios*) date from the 1950s. This shortcoming has been mirrored by a rapid growth in private-sector management training provision in the past decade. Private-sector establishments operate outside any effective regime of state supervision, and their qualifications and standing depend almost entirely on the reputation they have built up. Around 100 organisations are thought to offer MBAs.

In all, there are 957 registered private training companies and schools, of which seventeen are business schools. The remainder specialize in particular services, including consultancy, management training, technical training, training in information technology, commercial training, and language training. By frequency, the most common courses are in IT, human resources, general management, technology and communications. Most courses last for less than fifty hours, a large proportion are of no duration, and only a small proportion involve training of more than 300 hours.

The leading business schools are located in Madrid, Barcelona and Bilbao. Most are independent, and in recent years there have been various moves to organize them into associations. The Madrid Business School (84 per cent owned by the Banesto bank) offers two-year MBA programmes taught in English following the criteria of the American Assembly of Collegiate Schools in Business. Other well known schools follow the guidelines of the European Foundation for Management Development, and offer MBAs taught in Spanish – for example, IESE or ESDEN in Madrid and EADE and ESADE in Barcelona. These are part of the Asociación Española de Representantes de Escuelas de Dirección de Empresas (AEEDE), along with schools such as the Escuela de Organización Industrial (EOI), ESIC, ICADE, the Instituto de Empresa in Madrid and ESTE in San Sebastián. The most important school in the Basque country is DEUSTO in Bilbao. AEEDE is at present trying to regularize courses and qualifications in what continues to be a burgeoning market for such establishments. Some 90 per cent of MBA postgraduate students pay their own fees. Of executives in post, around 80 per cent are financed by their employer. A typical MBA programme lasts 800 contact hours.

Other private-sector provision

There has also been recent growth of in-service courses (seminars or day-release). Typical are those of the Instituto de Formación Empresarial and the Institute of International Research, which both offer tailor-made courses for companies. In 1976 Consultores Españoles was formed by the confederation of savings banks (Confederación Española de Cajas de Ahorro) to offer the same service. It provides some 100 seminars a year for 150 companies, and offers masters programmes in human resources/personnel management, labour law, and technology.

Two sources – AFIDE (Asociación Española de las Asociaciones para la Formación y el Desarrollo en la Empressa) and the DIRFO (Directorio de Formación) – provide basic information on the training available in some 1,100 training schools, 14,000 courses and seminars and 900 specialized short courses (see Appendix).

In-company training – offered initially by groups such as Tea Cegos or Sema Group/Sofemasa – is now estimated to take up to 75 per cent of company training budgets.

Statutory employee rights

The Workers' Statute (article 22) gives employees a statutory right to unpaid time off to sit appropriate training examinations, and the right to preference in choice of shifts when following regular study courses leading to academic or vocational qualifications. They also have the right to modify working time in order to attend training courses. This article also enjoins collective agreements to specify how the rights will be applied in practice. Article 64 of the Workers' Statute also gives the works council the right to be consulted on the company's training plans.

Agreed training provision

Both industry-level and company collective agreements provide for supplementary training arrangements, some of which are targeted at specific groups whilst others seek to raise the overall level of training.

Training for women

The national chemicals agreement recommends that companies should organize training courses for female employees.

Joint regulation

Several agreements establish joint committees to propose and implement company-level training. The chemicals agreement provides for joint bodies to draw up training plans aimed at easing adjustment to new technology and facilitating staff development. At Repsol, a chemical company with its own agreement, a committee consisting of three management and three trade union members is established in each workplace to draw up and monitor training programmes. At the power generator Unión Eléctrica Fenosa vocational training programmes are designed jointly by workers' representatives and management, concentrating mainly on retraining and updating: courses may be obligatory should management so decide.

The agreement at another power concern, Iberduero, commits both company and employees to participate in and develop training courses via a 'strategic training plan' drawn up after consultation with workers' representatives and subject to quarterly reports.

Retraining

At Fujitsu (computers) retraining for staff whose posts are threatened with redundancy is a company obligation, as is retraining for employees declared permanently and completely unfit for normal employment.

Time off

At Renault-Fasa, employees with at least two years' service are permitted up to four hours' weekly unpaid leave to attend appropriate training courses; the company also undertakes to join with workers' representatives in the provision of training courses. A stated aim is that all employees who wish to do so may be able to attend appropriate technical training courses out of working hours.

Distance learning

Administrative and technical employees at Unión Eléctrica Fenosa can participate in distance learning schemes established by the company in order to gain qualifications needed for promotion, with up to ten days off a year to pursue them.

Financial commitment

Agreed financial commitments can be in the form of a pledge either to spend an agreed percentage of the pay bill on training or to support individual employees undergoing training. For example, the tobacco company Tabacalera has agreed to dedicate 2 per cent of the pay bill to training, largely to facilitate individual promotion. Ford allows employees paid leave to take intermediate or higher-level examinations. It also pays up to Pta 75,100 (£440) per annum for higher education fees or expenses or Pta 44,630 (£262) for lower-level education expenditure, provided the employee is successful in assessments. At Mapfre, an insurance company, employees may be granted up to Pta 27,000 (£158) per annum towards the cost of fees and study for courses up to university preparatory level and up to Pta 41,000 (£241) per annum for higher education courses, provided that applicants have passed at least 50 per cent of the previous level of the course they are following. At Sanyo Fisher (electronics) employees with at least two years' service may apply for a 50 per cent subsidy towards the cost of vocationally related study, with a further 50 per cent reimbursement of fees on successful completion of study.

Telefónica (telecommunications) has a complex structure of training programmes which absorb, by agreement, not less than 5 per cent of the total wage bill. At Fujitsu external short training courses for staff development will be 70 per cent paid for by the company. The company will also pay 50 per cent of the costs of external courses relevant to the employee's professional development. The company will reimburse the cost of language classes in the Escuela Oficial de Idiomas, and can propose that selected employees attend classes in English or other relevant foreign languages, 70 per cent subsidized by the company.

In contrast, at Unión Explosivos Rio Tinto (chemicals) employees who have received training at the firm's expense are required to remain with the company for two years after training or repay the cost of training.

Funding

INEM traning schemes are financed by joint contributions from employers and employees. Employers contribute 0·6 per cent of basic pay and employees 0·1 per cent of basic pay. The government is currently proposing to raise the employer's contribution to 1·4 per cent, to finance a new continuous training initiative.

Appendix 10.1 Organizations

Ministry of Labour and Social Security (Ministerio de Trabajo y Seguridad Social):
Agustín de Bethencourt 4
28003 Madrid
tel. + 34 1 253 6000/253 7600
fax + 34 1 233 2996

INEM (Instituto Nacional de Empleo, the national employment institute):
Calle Condesa de Venadito 9
28027 Madrid
tel. + 34 1 585 9888
fax + 34 1 268 3981/268 3982

Asociación Española de Directores de Personal (AEDIPE: Spanish Association of Personnel Directors):
Moreto 10
28010 Madrid
tel. + 34 1 468 2217

DIRFO (Directorio de Formación)
Calle Orense 28 8°c
28020 Madrid
tel. + 34 1 556 7956
fax + 34 1 556 7912

AFIDE (Asociación Española de las Asociaciones para la Formación y el Desarrollo en la Empresa)
Calle Encarnación 132–134 4°
Barcelona
tel. + 34 32 13 2968
fax + 34 32 10 8901

Confederación Española de Organizaciones Empresariales (CEOE: the Spanish employers' organization):
Diego de León 50
28006 Madrid
tel. + 34 1 563 9641
fax + 34 1 262 8023

Unión General de Trabajadores (UGT):
Hortaleza 88
Madrid
tel. + 34 1 308 3333

Comisiones Obreras (CC.OO):
Fernández de la Hoz 6
28010 Madrid
tel. + 34 1 419 5454

Further reading: comparative and European information

CEDEFOP (European Centre for the Development of Vocational Training)

CEDEFOP, the European Community organization responsible for fostering the exchange of information and experience in the field of vocational training, publishes a variety of materials on national education and training systems (usually with an English-language edition), and has been the body responsible for co-ordinating the EC programme on the comparability of vocational training qualifications. A list of publications can be obtained from CEDEFOP, Jean Monnet House, Bundesallee 22, 1000 Berlin 15, Germany (tel. + 49 30 88 41 20, fax + 49 30 88 41 22 22). CEDEFOP publications can also be ordered in the UK through HM Stationery Office, and through national official distributors in other EC member states.

National Institute of Economic and Social Research (NIESR)

NIESR has carried out comparative research on vocational education and training, in particular concentrating on UK, German and French experience. Areas covered since the mid-1980s include: intermediate skills, the training of foremen, training in the hotel sector, in woodworking, in the clothing industry and in retailing. Results have been published in the NIESR's *National Economic Review*. NIESR, 2 Dean Trench Street, Smith Square, London SW1P 3HE (tel. 071-222 7665).

Education and training systems

VAN RESANDT (ed.), *A Guide to Higher Education Systems and Qualifications in the European Community*, Kogan Page, 1991.

TONY RABAN, *Working in the European Communities*, Hobson, 1988. A guide to higher education systems and graduate recruitment practices.

RICHARD ROSE and GÜNTER WIGNANEK, *Training without Trainers: how Germany avoids Britain's supply-side bottleneck*, Anglo-German Foundation, 1990.

JOHN BYNNER and KEN ROBERTS (eds.), *Youth and Work: transition to employment in England and Germany*, Anglo-German Foundation, 1992.

DEPARTMENT OF EDUCATION AND SCIENCE, *Aspects of Vocational Education and Training in the Federal Republic of Germany*, HMSO, 1991.

ORGANIZATION FOR ECONOMIC CO-OPERATION AND DEVELOPMENT, *Education at a Glance: OECD indicators*, OECD, Paris, 1992.

Managers

NATIONAL ECONOMIC DEVELOPMENT COUNCIL (NEDO), *The Making of Managers*, NEDO, 1987. A report on the training and development of managers in the United States, West Germany, France, Japan and the UK.

JEAN-LOUIS BARSOUX and PETER LAWRENCE, *Management in France*, Cassell, 1991.

CHRISTEL LANE, *Management and Labour in Europe*, Edward Elgar, Aldershot, 1989. Contains chapters on vocational training and managers in the UK, France and Germany.

PETER LAWRENCE, *Managers and Management in West Germany*, Croom Helm, 1980.

ALISON ALSBURY, *European Executive Training*, FT/Pitman, 1992. A guide to short courses held in English for executives in European business schools and universities. Although covering primarily UK institutions, the guide includes courses at INSEAD, Erasmus University, HEC (Jouay-en-Josas, France), EAP, IMD (Lausanne), the Irish Management Institute and USW (Germany).

IPM PUBLICATIONS ON THE EC

The IPM produces two publications to keep personnel practitioners informed and up to date on the EC:

THE SINGLE EUROPEAN MARKET AND PERSONNEL MANAGEMENT:

Executive Brief

A summary of the impact of the EC on employment regulation and personnel policy covering EC employment law, the Social Charter, key personnel issues and how the EC works, with sources of further information.

The *Executive Brief* is updated every 3–4 months.
Price: £5 IPM members: £12 non-members

IPM EC UPDATE

Monthly Brief

IPM's *EC Update* is a monthly brief on all the latest EC developments and issues affecting the personnel professional, including:

* progress on the Social Charter Action Programme
* EC employment laws
* free movement of workers within the EC
* health and safety issues
* equal opportunities
* training
* the EC employment situation
* recent publications and forthcoming conferences of interest
* copies of relevant EC documents

A free copy of the EC *Executive Briefing* mentioned above is included with the first issue.

Price for annual subscription: £72 IPM members; £120 non-members

---

To order:

Please send cheques with order, with membership number if member, to Liz Byrne, Secretary EC Affairs, Institute of Personnel Management, IPM House, 35 Camp Road, Wimbledon, SW19 4UX.

Both publications are produced by Cherry Mill, IPM's Policy Adviser, EC Affairs.